MORNING SHADOWS, EVENING SUN

MORNING SHADOWS, EVENING SUN

Stories of Namibia's Professional Hunters

BY

Brad Fitzpatrick

Safari Press Inc.

Fitzpatrick, Brad

Second edition

Safari Press

2014, Long Beach, California

ISBN 978-1-57157-412-1

Library of Congress Catalog Card Number: 2012953085

10 9 8 7 6 5 4 3 2 1

Printed in China

Readers wishing to receive the Safari Press catalog, featuring many fine books on big-game hunting, wingshooting, and sporting firearms, should write to Safari Press Inc., 15621 Chemical Lane, Huntington Beach, CA, 92649-1506, USA. Tel: (714) 894-9080 or visit our Web site at www.safaripress.com.

This book is dedicated to
Namibia's professional hunters,
and
to my wife, Bethany,
for her support throughout
the writing of this book.

TABLE OF CONTENTS

Foreword

My first awareness of South-West Africa—the country we now know as Namibia—came from reading Jack O'Connor's account of hunting there with his wife, Eleanor, in the early 1970s. At that time, the safari industry was still centered in East Africa. Safaris were longer then, and most game lists included dangerous game. The concept of a shorter hunt for plains game was almost unheard-of, and the southwestern corner of the continent was an out-of-the-way place visited by very few Americans. O'Connor made it sound like an enjoyable hunt in a wonderful place, so I added South-West Africa to the places I wanted to see.

Not too many more years passed before I made that dream a reality. I first hunted there in 1979, on my third African safari. It was still South-West Africa, still a quiet backwater, still a place visited by few Americans. By then I had read James Mellon's *African Hunter,* and I knew a lot more about the country. I understood its roots as a German colony, and I knew it was a popular destination for Europeans, especially those who spoke German. As a young hunter, I appreciated its affordability. Although it was still not a dangerous-game destination, I enjoyed its rocky hills and broad valleys, and I had a fantastic experience hunting for kudus, gemsboks, springboks, and mountain zebras.

Much to my surprise, it wasn't just that few Americans had visited this fine country. Very few were even interested. In the 1970s and on through the 1980s, you could hardly give away a South-West African safari in the United States. Back then I hunted with Ben Nolte, one of the finest professional hunters I have ever been with, and I expected him to have a long and bright future in the outfitting industry. It was not to be; business was so slow that, in time, he gave up and went back to ranching livestock.

(Photo courtesy of Jacques Strauss/Kowas Safaris)

His two sons are now professional hunters, enjoying the success that their father dreamed of—and that indicates how much things have changed for the new Namibia as opposed to the old South-West Africa. Back then, the hunting was excellent, but the species were limited and the places where good hunting could be found were far fewer. Today there must be more than ten times the wildlife in Namibia than when I first hunted there thirty-one years ago. The available species have at least doubled, if not trebled. Once-scarce animals such as blue wildebeests and elands are now commonplace. Antelopes such as sables, roans, and waterbucks remain prized, but are no longer rare. Non-natives, including impalas, blesboks, and black wildebeests, are now practically endemic.

In 1979, only remnant mountain zebra populations remained along the spine of the Erongo Mountains. Today these animals are widespread and plentiful, as are common zebras. It is not only the plains game that has benefited. In 1979, even the sight of a leopard track was cause for remark (and, in those days, some concern). Today both leopards and cheetahs are widespread. Elephants continue to increase in the far north, producing good ivory. Elephant hunting is no longer a limited and highly specialized endeavor, but simply part of the Namibian safari scene. Buffaloes and lions remain highly restricted in both quota and range, but both can be hunted in modern Namibia, and quality is excellent. White rhinos, too, can be hunted, and Namibia and South Africa are the only two countries on the continent to which CITES has awarded a black rhino quota. No longer a sleepy backwater, Namibia now has a powerhouse safari industry that, continent-wide, is second only to South Africa's.

It is not entirely clear how this sea change came about. I presume to take no credit. I wrote widely and avidly about South-West African hunting toward the end of the 1970s and on through the 1980s. Several

(Photo courtesy of Jacques Strauss)

of my colleagues did as well, but it had seemingly little effect. South Africa's game ranching and hunting industry blossomed when Kenya closed and the safari industry moved south. If Namibia benefited from this, then it was a delayed reaction! Perhaps it was a matter of persistence, rather than any one event or chain of events. For whatever reason, the market developed. With hunting tourism growing, the safari industry grew as well. More land was converted from livestock to game. More investments were made in breeding stock, long-gone species were re-established, and new species were introduced.

Although Namibia is, along with South Africa, one of just two countries where the entire Big Five can be hunted, Namibia remains primarily a plains-game destination. In today's safari market, however, this is no longer a negative since the vast majority of all modern African hunts are plains-game safaris. Hunting in modern Namibia retains the same charm it offered as South-West Africa: beautiful scenery and perfect climate; excellent accommodations and competent, qualified professional hunters; superb road network, infrastructure, and logistics; and rates that remain affordable. The big difference today is that there are many more animals in many more places!

In 1979, the game was much more scattered. Although there might be a base of operations, it was common to go to a certain area for specific animals: into the Erongos for zebras; out to the edges of the Namib or the Kalahari for springboks and gemsboks; to the far north for elands, blue wildebeests, and waterbucks. Today one might go to specific areas to find particularly high-quality specimens of any given animal, but most hunting properties now offer a wide variety of game in a single area.

Much credit must be given to the ranchers and professional hunters who persevered through lean years and made all this happen. This book is a collection of their stories: Namibian hunting as told by the professional hunters who have lived it and make their living by it. Although some of the contributors would be the same, this is not a book that could have been marketed thirty years ago, when so few of us had any interest in their part of Africa. Today, it is a most timely book

(Photo courtesy of Jacques Strauss)

as Namibia is emerging as a premier safari destination, an eclectic mix of thornbush, desert, mountain, and, in the Caprivi, even swamp. This is a country that beckons to the first-time African hunter in search of the short plains-game safari. Namibia beckons equally to the veteran in search of a local rarity such as a Damara dik-dik or a black-faced impala, or perhaps an animal that has eluded him elsewhere such as a leopard or a big sable. Namibia truly has it all, and the international community of sportsmen and women has long since recognized this.

This collection is not only timely, but it is an invaluable addition to the rich literature of Africana. You see, as popular as Namibia has become, there are very few books in English dedicated to this important safari destination. Honestly, I wish I'd thought of it! But it's just as well. Namibia is not a new destination, but her robust safari industry is new, and Brad Fitzpatrick is of a new generation of outdoor writers, versatile and innovative as well as talented. He has created a book we will all enjoy reading, one that will teach us much about a great hunting country with a strong hunting industry. Sit back, imagine you have a cold Windhoek Lager at hand, and enjoy *Morning Shadows, Evening Sun.*

Craig Boddington
Elk City, Kansas
August 2010

Introduction

It is dark outside the window of the airplane except for the flashing blue strobe on the wing. The cabin is filled with the roar of the engines. Thirty-five thousand feet below, veiled in darkness, is the interior of the African continent. No lights can be seen in the dark wilderness. For a passenger on the overnight flight from Germany to Windhoek, the only means of pinpointing a location is on the small video screens placed throughout the cabin, which show a path traced longitudinally from Europe south toward Namibia.

There is no sound in the cabin except the motors; the passengers are mostly asleep in the hours just before dawn. Not you. You are bound for Africa, destined to set foot in the ancient sands and hunt wild game on untouched land that looks much as it did a thousand years ago: a wilderness of thorns and rocks and vast plains that appear dark and brittle in the dry winter months. Through the windows on the left side of the plane, you can see a dim lightening of the eastern horizon. Slowly the daylight grows, and soon, in the tangerine glow, like a fire at the edge of the earth, you can see the bulge of the rising sun. Far below, you see Africa for the first time in your life.

As the sun illuminates the landscape, you can see Namibia's Atlantic coastline and the white-capped waves that are driven up from Antarctica by the cold Benguela Current. This great stream flows northward along the southwestern coast of Africa and causes an upwelling in the sea that makes the waters off Namibia some of the most fertile in the world. Along the stark Skeleton Coast, these cold currents fall against the sand of the world's oldest desert, the Namib. Frigid ocean waters turn into mountains of sand that stretch eastward, deep into the interior of the country. From your small port window in the plane, you can see the skeletal remains of wooden ships broken and festooned at the edge of the sea. Their hulls were left to bleach in the sun as a reminder of the ironic fate met by their crews: shipwrecked after a journey across the ocean, only to perish of dehydration in the featureless coastal deserts.

The plane tilts toward the rising sun, and the dunes are replaced by stark, gray mountains that rise up in the center of the country, looking very much as though the sand has suddenly petrified and turned to jagged cliffs. At sunrise, these interior mountains, some of the highest in all of Africa, cast long shadows in the morning light. It is a hard land that offers neither respite for the weak nor reprieve for the unfit. Farther inland, however, the rocky earth blends with vast plains of thornbush and dry grass that form the bulk of the nation's central highlands. Here you see game trails, cut by generations of grazing animals as they navigated the paths that led to food and water and cover. The only roads you see in the interior, other than the few dead-straight two-tracks linking the sparsely populated villages, were carved not by humans but by the wild herds that have adapted over millennia to live in this harsh and unforgiving landscape.

There are few places that exist in a more natural state than the young nation of Namibia. Its vast open spaces, many of which have never been touched by humans, stretch from the beaches of the western coastline all the way to the interior of the Kalahari Desert. At the country's extreme north is a narrow finger of land traded to the colonizing Germans by the British Empire, the Caprivi Strip. The great Kwando River bisects the strip, and the abundance of water from the region's rivers and pans creates a green oasis in an otherwise dry land. In Namibia's extreme south lie miles of country dominated by weathered rock pilings and scattered forests of fan-shaped quiver trees.

Since its period of German colonial rule in the early twentieth century, Namibia has been a place where humans must continuously test themselves against the will of nature. Summers are hot and water is scarce. The winters are cold, and the great cattle herds that were originally brought into the country to feed the colonists quickly perished from disease and predation by wild animals. The early

(Photo courtesy of Jacques Strauss)

colonists learned that game, although it competed with domestic stock, was much easier to manage than cattle. Wild animals were largely immune to the diseases that killed cattle. Oryxes, kudus, springboks, and hartebeests had all adapted to the harsh countryside and could find food and water and avoid predators without the help of humans. Soon, the German colonists were tied to the wild herds for their very survival.

This appreciation for wildlife has made Namibia a country that has long been perfecting the concept of utilizing and managing wild game herds despite the fact that it is one of the world's youngest nations. With the rise in the number of international sport hunters throughout the twentieth century, Namibia became a model for effective game ranching and the intelligent use of wildlife. As the bulk of the safari industry shifted from concessions in the former British colonies to game ranches in southern Africa in the late twentieth century, Namibia became the first nation to pioneer the concept of communal conservancies: areas where wild game was managed by local communities. A proclamation declaring the need to manage and conserve wildlife is even written into the country's constitution.

Today, Namibia stands at the forefront of managing wildlife through sport hunting to benefit not only local communities, but the game itself. NAPHA, the association of Namibia's professional hunters, acts as the voice of the nation's sportsmen. In modern Africa, where the ever-growing need to satisfy the burgeoning human population places greater demands on limited resources, Namibia has learned to effectively and efficiently utilize wild game while conserving those same populations for future generations. Namibia's professional hunters are pioneers—authors who are writing the next chapter in the book of Africa's sporting and conservation history.

The sun has risen over the dry plains, and the vast heart of Namibia lies spread out from one horizon to the next as the plane descends, listing slightly as it nears the runway. The engines slow and the earth grows larger and more detailed through the window until the wheels hit the tarmac and the plane taxis toward the tall, square, glass-fronted entrance to Hosea Kutako International Airport. This is what you have come for. This is Africa.

CHAPTER I

The Cats of Sangwali

Professional hunter: Allan Cilliers
Location: Caprivi

It was just before midnight when two male lions crossed the border of Mamili National Park in northern Namibia and slipped over the edge of Sangwali Village in the moonlight. Under the shadows of palms, the lions moved without a sound over the midnight-blue sand, following the scent of cattle like sharks trailing the aroma of blood in an ocean current. They passed through the tall reeds that grew on the flood plain, moving shoulder-to-shoulder and without a sound over the warm sand until they came to the edge of Sangwali and stopped under the drooping veil of a broken palm. With the open plain behind them, the two males stood panting silently in the heat of the night, studying the sleeping village.

Sangwali was a series of small huts spread out in a clearing at the edge of the forest. The small homes were lined up in a row along the single-lane dirt track, their roofs and walls made of rusting corrugated tin. At that late hour nothing stirred, and the village was silent. The lions, likely brothers, were drawn forward by the scent of the cattle sleeping behind the plank rails of a kraal, a pen where livestock is gathered during the night to keep the herd safe from predators. On that night, however, the flimsy planks did nothing to stop the two lions. The big males started across the open flood plain, the largest breaking into a steady trot and then a canter as it reached the edge of the kraal. With a shocking level of grace given its almost quarter-ton bulk, the lion leaped cleanly over the fence and landed among the sleeping cattle inside the walls of the wooden enclosure. The cat stood within the ranks of the herd, its tail lashing as it looked at the herd with eyes capable of seeing in the near-total darkness.

The silence of the night turned into a chorus of bellows and a roar of thumping hoofs as the herd rose at once and charged blindly around the confines of the kraal in a desperate effort to escape. The panicked

Lions still roam throughout much of the Caprivi Strip and sometimes come into conflict with man. (Photo courtesy of Jofie Lamprecht)

cattle broke free of the enclosure and ran through the moonlit grass, bellowing as they rushed along the edge of the huts where the villagers slept and across the flood plain into the darkness. The lion that had leaped the fence bore down on the fleeing herd from behind, closing the gap with each stride. Its brother came at full speed from the left flank, eyes flashing in the moonlight, and the two lions converged on the scrambling cattle as they bellowed and ran blindly into the darkness.

The larger male gathered itself, coiling its legs below it and then extending to full length as it caught one of the heifers and pulled it over in a thrashing pile in the sand. Soon the lion had its throat, and its brother caught hold of the flank. The cats held their grip, lying motionless side-by-side and growling in the moonlight until the heifer relaxed and lay still in the short grass, steam rising from its fresh wounds. As the cow breathed its last, the villagers of Sangwali gathered, assembling at the edge of the line of huts. Shouting among themselves and lighting torches, they looked over the splintered rails of the kraal. When they had assembled most of the men in town, they set out into the darkness, shouting and waving their torches at the two lions. The cats finally lost their nerve, and with rumbling growls and snarls, they left their kill and vanished into the night.

Sangwali village is located within a few kilometers of Mamili National Park in Namibia's East Caprivi region. The park is bordered on the west by the muddy Kwando River and on the east by the Linyanti River. The southern border of the park lies just across the Kwando from Botswana's vast Okavango Delta, an alluvial flood plain that stretches out in a series of fingerlike riverbeds that drain into the sands of the Kalahari Desert. Much of Mamili's western boundary along the Kwando River is a vast flood plain dominated by grasses that can exceed the height of a man during the rainy season. Unlike most of Namibia, Mamili has a good supply of water for most of the year, and because of this, species that are absent throughout much of the country—lechwes, buffaloes, hippos, and crocodiles—thrive in the region. It is also home to a sizable portion of the nation's wild lion population.

The lions of Caprivi are very large and have similar genetics to the lions of the Okavango, a region that is renowned for producing some of the largest cats ever entered into the record books. The lions of Caprivi are also among the most aggressive in Africa because they live in proximity to villages and ranches and are often harassed by livestock owners and their dogs. A sizable portion of the region's estimated 160,000 cattle fall victim to marauding lions each year, and retaliation by livestock owners in the form of thrown rocks and rifle shots has left the lions in the region particularly willing to attack when confronted.

Professional hunter Allan Cilliers knew something of confrontations with lions. A former game ranger in Etosha National Park and the Kavango and Caprivi regions, Cilliers had faced cattle-killing lions on several occasions and knew just how deadly such an encounter could be. Cilliers, a tall, full-bearded man with a year-round tan from hours spent under the Namibian sun, had been one of the first mounted rangers in Etosha before he switched careers and became a professional hunter.

In August 1998, Cilliers was guiding hunting safaris in the eastern Caprivi when he was notified that the Ministry of Environment and Tourism (MET) had issued two problem-lion permits for the big males that had been killing cattle in villages along the border of Mamili National Park. Cilliers had the right to hunt in all of the eastern Caprivi, an area covering eleven thousand square miles of flood plains, mopane woodlands, and palm thickets. Opportunities for problem-lion permits in the region were rare. When Cilliers received word that the permits were available, he notified his safari client, Phil Netznick. Cilliers told his client that two male lions had killed nine cattle in less than a month in the villages of Sauzuo, Mbambazi, Samudono, and Sangwali, and that the cats had been offered on problem-control licenses by the government. They would have to track the lions on foot through the palm forests along the Kwando River, a dangerous and difficult proposition. Netznick agreed to hunt the lions. After Netznick arrived at Cilliers's camp, they gathered equipment and supplies and then set out for Sangwali.

In the heat of midday, the carcass of the cow swarmed with metallic blue-and-green Calliphoridae, carrion flies. They buzzed around the uneaten flesh on the cow's flank as Cilliers rubbed his bearded chin and surveyed the kill. He thought it was strange that the lions had not come back to feed on the cow, but that had been their habit with the other kills they had made in the weeks leading up to their arrival in Sangwali. The two lions ate very little from the carcasses of the cattle they killed and often left their kills to the scavenging jackals and hyenas that followed them through the moonlight.

The carcass of the cow they found had been dragged from a nearby village and partially eaten on the nearby flood plains. Cilliers read the tracks and knew that the lions were large males; based on the fact that they had developed such a close alliance, they were likely brothers. They seemed to have no reason to kill so frequently and did so in spite of an abundance of natural prey. Because they ate only sparingly of the kills, Cilliers knew that baiting the lions was not going to be an effective option since the cats were not likely to return once they abandoned their kill.

The lion spoor was four days old, and Cilliers knew that following the tracks would be futile. He had met his Ju/'hoansi Bushman trackers, Tsissiba and Gau, while working as chief game ranger in the Kavango district fourteen years before, and they studied the spoor as they smoked hand-rolled cigarettes in the shade of a withered palm. The Ju/'hoansi of northern Namibia still live very much as their ancestors did, hunting and traveling through the vast Kalahari on foot in search of game, which they kill with poisoned arrows. As a nomadic hunting tribe, the Ju/'hoansi have developed tracking skills that are legendary, but even Gau and Tsissiba were unable to unwind the tangle of four-day-old tracks.

Since baiting would be fruitless and the spoor was too old to follow, the hunting party would have to figure out another way to locate the

Allan Cilliers, on the left, served as a game ranger in Etosha before becoming a professional hunter. (Photo courtesy of Allan Cilliers)

cats, or they would have to wait until the lions reappeared and killed once more. Cilliers and Netznick set out in search of fresh spoor near Sangwali, and Allan sent Gau and Tsissiba east onto the flood plain in an effort to pick up the tracks of the marauding lions as they crossed into or out of Mamili Park. On their first afternoon in Sangwali, Cilliers and Netznick set out from town in the hunting car and drove the narrow two-track roads that crossed the palm forests and reedy plains, hoping to find fresh spoor or a recent kill.

For some time it appeared that the lions had moved out of the area, but on the fourth day Cilliers received word from his trackers that they had located fresh spoor along the banks of the Kwando near the village of Sauzou. The tracks had been left the night before as the cats crossed back into the communal lands outside the park, and the experienced Ju/'hoansi had little trouble following the spoor across the sandy soil of Caprivi. Cilliers and Netznick double-checked their big rifles and the hunting party set out, moving from one palm thicket to the next. The Bushmen bent over the track while Cilliers and Netznick covered the trail ahead with their heavy guns.

At dusk, the spoor led down to the banks of the Kwando and disappeared into the churning brown water. Cilliers and the others stood on the bank of the river, the western horizon a deep red, and looked into the forest on the other side. The lions had crossed the river into Botswana. There was nothing more they could do.

The men returned early the next morning after tea and cigarettes. In the first gray light of dawn, the hunters worked their way along the muddy banks of the Kwando within earshot of a herd of hippos that had recently returned to the river after a night of foraging on the bank. The hippos lounged in the water like so many granite boulders in the dim light. Keeping a close eye on the loafing hippos, Allan and the others searched for any sign that the lions had returned.

Tsissiba paused and studied a wet blade of grass that was sprinkled with drying sand. Gau joined him and they crossed back and forth over the area for some time, talking quietly to each other and pointing to the earth with long, thin reeds. Now and then one or the other would motion toward a patch of wet earth on the bank. Finally they turned to Cilliers, who was still uncertain what they had found, and told him the lions had crossed back into Namibia. They had found the spoor. Cilliers never had cause to doubt his seasoned tracking team, but as they worked their way up the bank, moving one step at a time and pointing at broken blades of grass or single droplets of water drying in the morning light, he had his reservations. Two hundred yards from the water, however, they came upon the fresh tracks of two big male lions, their pug marks clearly visible in the soft red light of dawn.

Tsissiba and Gau led the hunters into the thorns on the trail of the two cats. The lions followed a meandering course through the waist-high grass under the palm canopies of the flood plain. High above, in the green fronds, songbirds raised their voices in a chorus of calls that welcomed the day as the men moved with grave alertness, the trackers bent low and talking only occasionally as they pointed to the spoor with their long sticks and gestured at the lion's path. Together the four men moved in close order through the cathedral of palms, Cilliers and Netznick covering each thicket with their heavy rifles as the heat of the day increased and the lions moved farther away from the river and into deeper cover near the villages where the cats had slaughtered cattle for months.

After five hours, Gau froze as if rooted in the sandy earth and fixed his gaze on the grass ahead. Cilliers scanned the bush ahead with his rifle at the ready—butt down, muzzle tilted out and forward— awaiting a charge the way a bobwhite hunter on a Georgia plantation might await the rise of a covey when the pointing dogs lock up. He pulled Netznick into position close beside him and circled Gau, who stood frozen, sweat on his face and flies circling his dark lips, watching the thornbush ahead. The cover was thick, and there were only a few shooting lanes among the drooping palms and tufts of thick-stemmed grass.

Thirty yards ahead, under an umbrella of palm fronds, Cilliers saw a portion of a lion's face and a lashing tail. The other big male was somewhere close—perhaps even closer than the one Cilliers could see. The first male was visible in fragments between the low-growing palms. Allan could see an ear and one of the lion's eyes appearing like pieces of a deadly puzzle in the dense cover. With a grunt, the lion was up and moving away through the palms, its brother rising from behind a veil of grass and trotting at the heels of the first cat until they were both swallowed by the heavy thorn. They appeared again two hundred yards away, moving at a gallop across the open flood plain before disappearing again into the thick green arms of low-growing palms on the other side of the savanna.

The men paused to collect themselves, all of them knowing that the outcome of the last five minutes would have been altogether different if the lions had opted to charge rather than retreat. They set out again on the spoor, the cats now fully aware that they were being pursued.

As midday stretched into evening and shadows tilted across the sand, the lions crossed the boundary into Mamili and the men were forced to stop. Cilliers knew that there was a very large, aggressive male lion that controlled a pride just inside the park's boundary, and he hoped the pride male would drive the two marauders back out of Mamili and into the communal lands where Cilliers and his men could resume the hunt. With the lions inside the park, the hunters would have to wait until morning.

After a night of restless sleep, Cilliers and the others returned to the place where they had been forced to abandon the lion's trail the night before. Gau and Tsissiba moved along the park boundary looking for any sign that the males were headed back toward the villages or the river. It was not long before they found what they were looking for: The spoor of both males showed where they had left the park the night before and headed directly back toward Sangwali. The cats entered the village early that morning and killed a chicken before the villagers gathered and drove the lions away, shouting and clanging steel pots together until the cats rose with a chorus of growls and trotted into the trees. The cats then moved toward Samudono Village and crossed the gravel and sand road that leads from Mamili to Katima Mulilo, the largest town in Caprivi and the jumping-off point for most safaris in that region.

As the lions crossed the Katima Mulilo Road, the terrain changed. The tall palms and reeds that dominated the flood plain were replaced by groves of mopane and thorn. Acacia and shepherd's trees rose above the tangled mopane and offered scant shade and browse to the herd animals that lived in the region. Long hours of tracking left the men exhausted, thorn torn, fly bitten, and reddened by the intense sun. The Ju/'hoansi remained in front throughout the hunt, pointing or gesturing in one direction or another as they read the spoor while Cilliers and Netznick guarded them against a sudden charge. As the sun rose and the midday heat intensified, Gau found a depression in the earth where the two males had lain to cool themselves in the sand. But the spindly acacia they chose did not provide enough shade to keep

Phil poses with one of the lions taken in Sangwali. (Photo courtesy of Allan Cilliers)

the lions cool, and soon the two cats moved deeper into the mopane in search of better shade.

Cilliers knew that the lions would not go much farther in the intense heat. He gathered the men close together, with Netznick at his right elbow and the trackers beside him. He ordered them to stay in tight formation and not to break ranks when the lions charged, which they likely would after being pursued into such dense cover. He made sure that the action of Phil's .470 double was tight and that the safety catch was on to prevent an accidental discharge while moving through the bush. In the thick, twisted cover where the lions were, there would be little room to shoot and absolutely no room for error. His last directive was simple: In the event of a charge, everyone was to stand his ground in spite of the primal compulsion to run away. Shoulder-to-shoulder, the mopane flies swarming their sweating faces, they moved as one into the lair of thorns where the cats were waiting for them.

A mile into the mopane, Gau waved his thin hand and stopped the group. He lowered himself close to the ground, his muscles taut as he studied a termite mound twenty yards ahead. Cilliers held his .458 Lott rifle close beside him as he scanned the mound and the gray piles of thorn just beyond it. There was a shepherd's tree to the right of the termite mound, and mopane bushes skirted the base of the tree. Cilliers scanned left and right, watching for any sign of the cats through the swarming halo of mopane flies that circled his face.

Both of the lions stood up behind the termite mound, not more than twenty yards from the men. They had been lying down, almost certainly flattening themselves in anticipation while listening to the men's approach. The pair stood with their tails lashing the air, growling deep within their chests. There was little time to make a decision. Cilliers studied both cats, turned to his client, and ordered Netznick to shoot the lion on the left.

The stillness of midday exploded with a thunderous clap and a flash of hot flame as Netznick touched off the right barrel of his .470 Nitro

Express. The lion on the left rose up and twisted in midair as the bullet raised a cloud of dust from its hip. Netznick had missed the shoulder with his first shot. The cat roared and spun in tight circles, disappearing behind the termite mound as the other lion broke parallel to the group, moving through the thick cover to Netznick's right before stopping with a grunt and turning back toward the men. The unwounded lion hesitated only a moment before lashing its tail straight over its back and charging—roaring and grunting as it bounded over the sand toward the men. Cilliers shouted for his client to empty his second barrel into the lion as Cilliers shifted his gaze between the two cats.

The charging male tipped its head back and gave a terrific snarling grunt as it came in a cloud of rising dust and shuddering mopane brush. Netznick fired again as the lion came into the opening where the men were standing. The five-hundred-grain bullet caught the lion too far back to be instantly fatal but it broke its spine, dropping the cat's rear half into the sand with a spray of dust. The lion continued forward on its front paws.

The first lion now rounded the lump of dry earth and came forward in a full rush at the men. Cilliers ordered Netznick to finish the other cat just as this one came, and Cilliers found the lion's great head over the open sights of his .458. The space between them was swallowed up in two great strides as the lion bore down on the group of men gathered close together. Cilliers held his sight picture, waiting until the lion's great head and flashing yellow eyes were within four yards before he pressed the trigger. The recoil of the .458 drove him backward as the lion collapsed and skidded to a dusty stop at his feet.

As Cilliers was finishing the first cat, Phil Netznick was frantically reloading his .470 double, breaking the action of the empty rifle and ejecting the empty brass as the lion with the broken spine continued forward on its front legs, snarling and growling. The action locked shut, and Netznick fired one last shot at ten feet that dropped the cat for good.

The whole attack had taken less than twenty seconds, but in that time the quiet mopane thicket had exploded into a dusty battlefield. With their ears still ringing and their eyes still scorched by a blend of dry, sandy air and nitrocellulose fumes, Netznick and Cilliers looked down at the two dead lions just beyond the toes of their boots. Netznick's lions were massive. The larger male weighed nearly five hundred pounds and was the largest lion ever killed in Namibia at that time. The second, smaller cat still ranked sixth in the record book. Cilliers inspected the lions and found that one of the males had been shot in the flank and the rear legs with buckshot. The wound had largely healed, but the irritation certainly had some influence on the lion's strong distaste for humans. The injury had not caused the lion to lose weight, and other than the healed buckshot wounds, both lions appeared to be in perfect health.

In addition to the impressive size of the cats, Netznick could take pride in the fact that he had earned his place in the record book by pursuing the big males honestly and at great personal risk. Allan Cilliers will be the first to tell you that there are few things in the world more risky than tracking problem lions in the thorn forests of Caprivi.

CHAPTER 2

A Stirring in the Water

Professional hunter: Jofie Lamprecht
Location: Caprivi

The Kwando River originates in central Angola near Mount Tembo and flows southward, forming a large portion of the border between Zambia and Angola before passing across Namibia's Caprivi Strip and into Botswana. When the river reaches northern Botswana, its main channel dissipates and the river forms the vast flood plains of the Linyanti Swamp, which, in turn, feed Botswana's Chobe region and form the Okavango Delta. In years of sufficient rainfall, the waters of the Linyanti spill over into the mighty Zambezi River. In dry years, the river simply vanishes into the sands of the Kalahari Desert, swallowed without a trace by the arid earth at the onset of the dry season.

The Caprivi region is unique to Namibia because it is the only portion of the country that receives large amounts of rainfall annually. The Kwando River acts as the boundary between the eastern and western halves of Caprivi, flowing southward one hundred miles to the west of Katima Mulilo, the largest city in the region. The Kwando and Okavango Rivers provide an abundance of fresh water, creating a lush, riverine habitat that is home to water-dependent species not found elsewhere in the country. Reedbucks, sitatungas, bushbucks, and lechwes are found there, as are great herds of Cape buffaloes that spend the mornings feeding out on the vast, green flood plains. Caprivi is home to large populations of both lions and leopards, and crocodiles sun themselves along the riverbanks. Hippos, which could not survive in any other part of the country, are found in great numbers in the papyrus jungles and twisting backwaters of the Kwando.

As in many other places in Africa, hippos are responsible for a large number of injuries and fatalities to humans in Caprivi each year. Caprivi residents are aware of the dangers hippos pose and do their best to avoid contact with them both on land and in the water, especially at night, when hippos come out onto the flood plains to feed and defend their favorite avenues to the water. On land, hippos become extremely aggressive, attacking any human unlucky enough to encounter them. During the day, hippos return to the water and remain relatively placid, although they are extremely territorial. Bulls in particular will even attack boats that enter their established territories.

It was a leopard, not a hippo, that brought professional hunter Jofie Lamprecht and his client to Caprivi. Although they had a good tom on bait at the onset of the hunt, the cat seemed to vanish, as leopards

Hippos are among Africa's deadliest animals, and are responsible for many human deaths each year. (Photo courtesy of Jofie Lamprecht)

so often do. On the second day of the hunt, Jofie led his client into the blind at two o'clock in the morning, but by eight o'clock there was no sign of the cat. Jofie suspected the leopard had either quit the bait or moved out of the area, so he decided that he and his client would set out after a hippo. Because the hippo was going to be given to the local residents, Jofie was allowed to use one of the boats belonging to the government Ministry of Environment & Tourism (MET).

The midmorning cruise on the Kwando served as a welcome relief from the hours spent cramped and motionless in the dark leopard blind. Malachite kingfishers passed over the boat, hunting for fish, and splendid carmine bee-eaters, a dash of color on their wings, dove at the surface of the river and plucked flies from the pools along the bank. On the open flood plain, herds of reedbucks and zebras fed on the new green grass, stopping to lift their heads and watch as the boat continued down the river.

The Kwando was lethargic and very clear, twisting through the flooded plains. In places, high walls of reeds and papyrus rose ten feet above the water on both sides like a dense green forest. Soon Jofie and his client saw their first hippos. The animals dropped their heads under the water as the boat approached. Only a stirring of bubbles and a swirling on the surface told the men that the hippos, each one weighing almost three tons, had passed almost directly under the MET boat as they escaped into the wall of reeds on the opposite bank.

This same scenario played out over and over again—the boat would turn a corner in the reeds and surprise the hippos with their heads above water just long enough for the client to raise his rifle, and then there would be nothing but a ripple on the surface as the hippos disappeared into the labyrinth of reeds and papyrus. By noon, Jofie and his client had traveled well downstream and had been offered little more than fleeting glimpses of hippos before they vanished.

Jofie changed tactics. At the next turn, a bull hippo dropped its massive head underwater, and Jofie ordered the boatman to kill power. The nose of the MET boat ran into the dense wall of reeds and stopped, rocking slowly with the gentle current as the men watched the water with their rifles ready. For some time, nothing appeared except a steady stream of small bubbles rising from the riverbed like carbonation in a bottle of seltzer water. They waited and watched, Jofie covering the surface with his .416 Remington Magnum in case the hippo opted to charge the boat.

Finally the bull's head broke the surface of the water, the small ears rotating as two geysers of water sprayed from its nostrils. Jofie leaned toward his client and told him to shoot because the bull would not remain on the surface for long. When the rifle cracked, the bull shook its head, sprayed, and dove deep into the water under its own power, instead of drifting slowly downward as it would have had it been hit in the brain.

The bull was coming back toward the boat underwater, a black shadow growing larger under the surface of the river. A rush of water preceded the bull and rocked the boat as the hippo powered through the water like a rotund submarine. When the bull reached the vicinity of the boat, it abruptly stopped, its black form positioned at the bottom of the river channel, almost underneath the boat. At once the bull began rising, driving like a torpedo up from the muddy bottom of the river toward the men on the surface. Through the clear water Jofie saw the bull's mouth, its jaws open.

A collision between the bull and the boat seemed imminent, and Jofie yelled to the men to brace themselves for the coming impact. An attack from directly below would almost certainly upset the boat, tossing the men into the water with the bull. Jofie watched the charging hippo over the iron sights of the rifle, feeling the sudden shudder as the bull's wake rocked the boat. As the gear began to slide across the flat rubber bottom, the hippo's front end passed under the boat like a black cloud heralding violent weather.

Jofie swung the rifle from one side of the boat to the other, trying to see the bull through the glare of sunlight on the surface and the

Professional hunter Jofie Lamprecht and his wife, Monica. (Photo courtesy of Jofie Lamprecht)

rising and falling waves. At any moment, he knew, the bull could rise up underneath them and topple the craft. Finally, as he moved to the starboard side of the boat, Jofie saw a dark form deep in the water directly below the boat. Squinting against the glare, Jofie could see the oblong head of the hippo. It was lying under the boat, facing to the right. Only its head was visible, which meant that the rest of the hippo's three-ton body was lying directly below and parallel to the boat. Jofie pointed the barrel of his rifle down until the muzzle almost touched the surface of the water, knowing the bull would have to lead a charge with its head and hoping his shot would connect before the bull could upset the boat and toss the men into the water.

Long seconds passed until the bull finally came for the boat again, driving straight up from the river bottom in a rush toward the men at the surface, jaws agape, teeth clearly visible in the wide, pink mouth. Jofie held his fire, watching the bull's rush over the rifle's sights and waiting until the hippo's great head broke through the surface of the river before he pressed the trigger and drove a four-hundred-grain solid into the oncoming bull with over five thousand pounds of energy. The bullet struck the hippo just behind the eyes, stopping it in midcharge and dropping it. In a slow descent, it wafted back down onto the muddy river bottom where it settled, dead at last.

Jofie worked the bolt and watched the bull over his sights. It was over. The boat was listing badly from the force of the bull's rush, but it did not overturn. The men had survived without receiving anything more than a wild spray of water when the hippo broke the surface and the 400-grain slug found its mark.

Because the great bull had settled at the bottom of the river, the true work now began. Jofie and his men would have to retrieve the bull from the water before they could begin butchering it, so first a rope would have to be attached to the bull, and then it would have to be pulled ashore through the heavy reeds. The men beached the boat and began the work of clearing reeds from the riverbank and securing the bull with a heavy line. At last they managed to fasten a heavy rope to

Jofie's client with the massive hippo bull that nearly capsized their boat. (Photo courtesy of Jofie Lamprecht)

the bull's great bulk and, with the help of villagers, began hauling the three-ton hippo toward the riverbank. The reeds made it difficult to pull the bull ashore, and they had to be cut away from the bank so that the hippo could be brought up, bit by bit, to where the butchering and celebration could begin. Soon a crowd had gathered, people standing with hands on hips and watching as the skinners pulled out their knives and began working on the old bull.

The hippo was the main entree for an impromptu festival that night on the banks of the Kwando. Thick strips of the rich, dark meat were carved and cooked over an open fire beneath the cloudless Namibian sky, and the celebration continued into the late hours, long after everyone had eaten and the fire had died away. The hippo's skull was taken for the celebration, so Jofie's client was not allowed to keep it even though it sported heavy ivory. Instead, the skull remains in the village on the banks of the Kwando, smooth and white, with one small, round hole drilled just between the bulging eye sockets. Losing the hippo skull was of little consequence to Jofie and his client, however, for when they returned to hunting near their camp they found that their luck with the leopard had changed. The old tom had returned to the bait, and was once again feeding.

CHAPTER 3

The Black and Blue Spoor

Professional hunter: Reinhard Mosich
Location: Erongo Mountains

Two hours' drive west of the capital city of Windhoek, Namibia's Erongo Mountains rise from the country's central plateau to an elevation of more than five thousand feet. This series of smooth, barren hills was formed when the inner chamber of a volcano collapsed inward during the late Mesozoic Era some one hundred million years ago. The lava chamber, with its igneous center, withstood the weathering that has reduced the volcano's outer walls. The remains of the lava form the irregular backbone of the Erongos.

Nearly a thousand years before the birth of Christ, San Bushmen sought shelter in the smooth overhangs and depressions in the rock. The labyrinth of tunnels and caves served as the center of San activity in the region. Ancient paintings on the rock walls of the Erongos depict scenes of San hunters pursuing a variety of game. Some of the animals in the paintings are ambiguous; the crude sketches of small antelopes are impossible to distinguish by species. But one recurring image is unmistakable: a large antelope with great horns that rise high above its head in corkscrew curls, an image that could only represent a big kudu bull.

Later, other tribes that settled in the area moved the San out of the Erongo Mountains and onto the fringe of the Kalahari. Today, the Erongo region is largely comprised of huge farms that cover tens of thousands of acres of savanna, acacia forest, and rocky hills. Many of the landholders have concluded that sport hunting is a viable and sustainable way to produce income, particularly because of the variety and quality of game that remains in the region. The Erongo region is one of the best places in Namibia to find a big leopard, as the rock escarpments and thick, thorny cover form prime habitat for cats. Each year, some of Namibia's largest leopards come from the region. It is also home to a good number of

Kudus are plentiful in the hills of central Namibia. Cover-loving and secretive, a big kudu bull is among the premier African trophies. (Photo courtesy of Hannes du Plessis)

endemic Hartmann mountain zebras and oryxes. And, as illustrated by the San more than three thousand years ago, the region is home to many large kudu bulls.

This species is the namesake of Reinhard and Stephanie Mosich's Erongo hunting farm, Kuduberg, which means Kudu Mountain in Afrikaans. Most of the farm is comprised of rocky hillsides with dense thorn cover. In the fall of 2007, however, wildfires swept down from the mountains and burned much of the vegetation off Kuduberg. The creeping wall of flame drove much of the game away from the farm and left Reinhard and Stephanie to do their best to find the few herds that remained in the unburned portions of the property. After the fires, the worst in over seventy years in the Erongo Mountains, a neighboring farmer offered Reinhard the opportunity to lead safaris on his farm—a testament to the good will of Namibia's landowners and the relationships that the owners of Kuduberg have formed with surrounding hunting farms. Reinhard's client, a hunter from the United States named Mike, arrived for the first safari on the new farm, and Reinhard immediately set out to locate the trophy Mike wanted most: a big tom leopard. It wasn't long before a large Erongo cat hit a bait that Reinhard had placed in the new hunting area, so the hunters built a blind in preparation for the cat's return.

Reinhard wanted Mike to rest during the day so he would be refreshed and prepared if the opportunity for a shot arose during the long evening in the blind. But Mike protested, wanting to take full advantage of his time on safari. Eager to set out after game, Mike convinced his PH to spend the afternoon hunting for antelopes in the Erongo foothills.

The hunters had already dropped off their supplies and gear in the blind, and the only rifle the two men had was Reinhard's 9.3x62 with four rounds of ammunition. Reinhard knew that Mike was a good shot who could place his bullet where he wanted it, and he trusted Mike not to take a shot he was unsure of, so he agreed to the afternoon hunt. The pair set out in search of game.

Kudus are large but are not normally considered dangerous; however, a wounded kudu bull badly injured Reinhard Mosich and left lasting impressions on the seasoned hunter. (Photo courtesy of Jacques Strauss)

It was not long before one of the region's big kudu bulls appeared out of a grove of low-growing acacia trees—a mature male sporting wide, brown, curling horns. The dark bull stood facing the men at the base of a rocky hill, lifting its head and great horns as it prepared for flight. Reinhard quickly set up the shooting sticks and gave his client the go-ahead to take the kudu.

Mike settled the rifle on the sticks and fired. The bull jumped and twisted at the shot before running into thick cover. It appeared to be hit hard, but Reinhard told his client to shoot again as the kudu galloped through the scattered brown thorns and low trees along the base of the hill. The second shot had no effect on the wounded kudu, which climbed the slope into heavier cover along one of the rocky ridges. Mike fired twice more, emptying the rifle, as the old kudu climbed into a thorn thicket higher up the slope and finally disappeared behind a wall of thorns and winter-brown grass. The rifle's final report echoed off the steep, gray walls and then faded into the evening silence.

The first shot had seemed good to Reinhard, and despite being without ammunition, he decided to have a look at the area where the bull had disappeared, hoping that the kudu would succumb to the effects of the first shot somewhere on the rocky slope. With the trackers leading the way, the hunters started up through the scattered boulders. It was rough going and difficult to negotiate, what with the loose stones and the creeping gray arms of wait-a-bit thorns that seemed to grow right out of cracks in the rock. On several occasions, the men tripped and fell to their knees as the scattered boulders clacked and rattled down the slope. Despite the difficult tracking conditions, the blood spoor remained constant.

Reinhard's trackers led the group up the slope, pausing to look over stones along the trail and pointing every so often to a splash of cranberry-colored blood on the rocks. The bull had been hit and was bleeding, but the hunters would have to hurry if they wanted to find their quarry before sunset.

The group tracked the kudu to a depression where they finally found it resting on its belly with its legs folded beneath its body and its heavy, deeply curled horns laid against its back. It appeared that the kudu would expire soon. Reinhard turned and with a wave of his hand motioned the men away from the place where the big bull was lying. He knew that if they left the bull alone it would likely die quickly, but if they approached it, it might spook and they would risk losing the kudu, for it was sure to continue up through the rocks toward the summit. If they lost the blood spoor in the darkness, they might lose the bull for good. Reinhard made the decision to go back to camp to get another rifle and allow the bull time to die. The men traced their way back down the face of the slope and returned to the main lodge at Kuduberg.

When they returned to the place where the kudu had been, Reinhard and his men found that the bull had risen from the narrow depression and moved off across the ridge. The hunters followed the scattered blood spoor into another rocky depression where they again found the old bull lying down, its head resting on the ground beneath the weight of its great horns. Reinhard watched the kudu for a moment, looking for any sign that the bull was still alive. There was none.

Reinhard turned to his client, told him that the bull was finished, and turned back to see the kudu suddenly on its feet. The bull stood wide-legged for a moment as though balancing itself on the loose rocks. Then, suddenly, the kudu lurched forward, lowered its head, and charged down the slope toward the hunters. Reinhard had only a moment to brace for the tremendous impact. The kudu bull ran directly into him, flattening him with its great weight. The other members of the party scattered and stood in disbelief, looking at the PH lying crushed on the rocks.

The bull had caught Reinhard along the ribs with the innermost curl of its horns and just above the base where the horns met. The great force had lifted the man off the ground before driving him several feet backward and dropping him back to the rocky earth. As Reinhard lay splayed on the loose granite boulders, the big bull renewed its attack, striking him with its crescent hoofs until one of the trackers fired three times, dropping the old bull across Reinhard's outstretched and bloodied body.

Reinhard was unconscious for a time, and when he awoke he felt a tremendous pain radiating through his left arm. Though Reinhard could not recall the impact that caused the injury, he knew his bicep was torn. The last thing Reinhard remembered was the shock of seeing the bull lower its head and charge. It was his client, his wife, and his trackers, all of whom witnessed the attack, who relayed the details to him.

The bull was skinned and taken back to camp. Despite being in tremendous pain, Reinhard insisted that his men drop Mike and him off at the leopard blind. It was not until Reinhard's head began to clear and the adrenaline wore off while sitting in the blind that he felt the worst of the pain and realized the full impact of the attack. His back stiffened, his legs ached, and the throbbing pain that radiated from his ripped bicep was terrific. Reinhard finally relented and called on the radio for his crew to come and get them. The leopard hunt would have to wait.

The spirals of a big kudu bull's horns form a perfect circle when viewed from the top. (Photo courtesy of Ben Gettinger/Crisp Photography)

By the following morning, Reinhard's wounds had turned various shades of violet and blue, especially across his chest, back, and lower legs. The force of the seven-hundred-pound bull bearing down on him had injured Reinhard badly, although he admits if it had been another species, such as an oryx, he would likely have been killed on its rapier horns. Instead, he was pitched and trampled by an antelope that many hunters consider to be docile and incapable of inflicting injury even when wounded. Reinhard would be the first to disagree with that statement.

Reinhard says there are many lessons to be learned from his experience with the kudu. One should never be without sufficient ammunition when in pursuit of game, and wounded animals should be left for a time before tracking begins. But most important is the lesson that so many of the Dark Continent's hunters have learned: Never underestimate the cunning, power, and tenacity of any African game animal. Kudu, which rarely make their way into discussions about dangerous game, have the size, speed, and power to inflict serious injuries. Reinhard Mosich can attest to that.

CHAPTER 4

The Race among the Rocks

Professional hunter: Gerard Erasmus
Location: Khomas Hochland

On most leopard hunts, the first task that must be accomplished when the hunter arrives in camp is to locate the pug marks of a big tom leopard. Fresh spoor indicates a cat is in the area, and the next step is to set out baits to draw it in and hold it until the hunter gets a shot. By the time professional hunter Gerard Erasmus picked his client up at Hosea Kutako Airport and drove the dusty miles back to his leopard-hunting camp in the Khomas Hochland, the hunt was ahead of schedule. Gerard had already found the spoor of a fantastic tom leopard. In fact, this particular tom had lived in the highlands for some time, roaming over a vast territory in the dry, hilly country and killing game and stock on surrounding ranches.

Gerard Erasmus is a professional hunter by trade, a specialist in finding big leopards. He has taken several outstanding cats that ranked high in the Namibian record books, hunting both over bait and with dogs. (Hunting leopards with hounds was a legal method until the laws were changed in 2009.) Even for an experienced leopard hunter like Erasmus, the size of this big tom's track was impressive. The pug marks, which were as big as postholes and almost as round, were pressed deep into the glossy quartz-sand riverbeds of the highlands each night as the leopard made its rounds in search of food.

The big male's territory overlapped that of several females in the area. Throughout the year, the tom moved around the perimeter of its range, keeping close watch over its mates, driving challengers out of the area, and killing as it pleased in the low valleys and rocky slopes. The dry hills and cool drainages were an ideal place for a leopard to survive long enough to reach the size that the old tom had attained.

Opportunistic by nature, the old leopard killed wild game and domestic stock interchangeably. The cat had not, however, taken any of the baits Gerard had offered it on previous hunts. As Gerard prepared

A handler takes a break during a leopard hunt with hounds. Outlawed in Namibia in 2009, leopard hunting with dogs was once standard. (Photo courtesy of Gerard Erasmus/ Sumsare Safaris)

for his client's leopard hunt, he placed baits that were hit by other leopards. He could not, however, tempt the old tom to take a meal.

This particular safari offered only a small window of opportunity to take the cat since the client would only be leopard hunting for ten days. After that, he and Gerard would board a plane and leave for Mozambique to hunt for Cape buffalo bulls in the coutadas bordering the Indian Ocean.

The hunters had several factors working against them when they set out to hunt the big tom. First, the old leopard had thus far simply refused any bait offerings. Perhaps, Gerard thought, the cat had been trapped once and had learned to recognize that food offerings from humans often came with a heavy price. Perhaps the cat knew how to recognize the characteristics of a food offering left by humans: the thick wires that knotted the meat to the base, the flurry of footprints left in the sand, and the faint, blended odors of sweat and gasoline left behind by the men's hands as they wired the bait.

In addition, the Khomas Hochland was facing a massive rabies epidemic. Sporadic rabies outbreaks across Namibia are not uncommon. Some are localized, but that year rabies had spread throughout the highlands. The animal most dramatically affected by rabies is the kudu. Whole herds can be wiped out as the disease spreads across an area, and that is what had happened the year Gerard and his client hunted for the big leopard in the Khomas Hochland. The rabies plague meant that there were dead kudu throughout the leopard's range. Between the kudu and the abundant livestock available on nearby cattle ranches, it was clear that getting the leopard to feed on bait and return to it during daylight hours was going to be extremely difficult.

Baiting for leopards in the Khomas Hochland is different from leopard hunting almost anywhere else in Africa. There are very few trees in the area, and the trees that do grow in the rocky soil are usually far too small to support a bait or a leopard, let alone both at the same time. Because of this, Gerard places his baits along dry riverbeds. Leopards have learned that it is easier to walk over a soft sand riverbed than to cut through acres of savage thorns while on patrol. Leopard tracks can also commonly be found on roads, but since there were far more dry rivers than roads in the highlands, Gerard concentrates his baiting efforts in the sandy riverbeds.

Gerard uses short bushes along the banks of the riverbeds to secure his baits. Heavy-gauge wire holds the zebra carcasses in place so that the leopards cannot haul them into the high, rocky cliffs that rise up from the river. Constructing blinds is tricky as well since there is only limited vegetation in the highlands, and any tall structure would draw the attention of the cats immediately. If the leopard struck one of the baits, Gerard would set about building a blind using the salmon-colored rocks and dry grass that grow in brittle yellow clumps on the hillsides.

As the safari began, there was no shortage of leopard tracks. Gerard's client, a fifty-three-year-old Texan, had gone to his doctor before leaving for Namibia to have his heart tested and blood work done. The doctor assured the man that he was fit enough for the miles of walking that might be required while searching for leopards in the highlands of central Namibia, a land of rockslides and steep slopes rising from the plains below. The steep terrain, combined with the four-thousand-foot elevation, meant that hunting in the Khomas would not be an easy task.

There was quite a bit of work to be done during the baiting process, including checking, setting, and replenishing baits that were in remote, rocky drainages far from any road. The mornings were cold and clear in the high mountains, and the work started well before dawn. Gerard woke his client early each day, and in the cold air their breath was visible in the firelight as the equipment was loaded into the truck. Throughout the day, the men traveled from one bait site to the next, examining the torn and tattered remains of dried flesh. By midmorning, the temperature rose and the mountains were hot and dusty. Flies swarmed over the baits as the men walked in circles studying the soft, cool sand in the shadowy riverbeds. There were plenty of leopards around and they fed regularly, but the old tom with the massive feet simply refused to touch the baits although its tracks were found frequently in the same riverbeds where baits were set.

Time was running short, and it became apparent to Gerard that the big leopard was not interested in dining on gifts of meat left wired to thornbushes along the dry riverbed. Each morning, its great round prints were found in the drainages, the only testimony to the cat's moonlit wanderings through the high, rocky hills. Gerard knew that it was time to switch tactics or they would never get a chance at the cat. In addition, local farmers had lost thousands of dollars of stock to this cattle killer and were demanding that something be done to stop the leopard before it bankrupted them.

Gerard called Roy Sparks on the sixth day of the leopard hunt. Roy, a veteran hunter and houndsman, was Namibia's dean of hound hunting

Preparing to set out on the spoor just after first light. The dry landscape and rocky hills made this leopard hunt particularly challenging. (Photo courtesy of Gerard Erasmus)

for leopards before the 2009 closure. Roy agreed that he would meet the hunters with his pack of leopard dogs the following morning.

Gerard sat down with his client over sundowners and explained the differences between baiting for leopards and hunting them with hounds. Hunts with hounds are challenging because the dry conditions in Namibia, particularly in the country's central and southern highlands, make it very difficult for hounds to trail cats once the thin topcoat of dew evaporates in the heat of day. As the sun set and the eastern horizon appeared like a belt of purple below the tangerine sky, Gerard explained how the houndsman and his handlers would work with the dogs while the client tried to get into position for a safe shot at the cat. The PH's job was to keep track of the dogs, the client, and the enraged leopard, a task only slightly less chaotic than conducting an orchestra on a sinking cruise ship.

Hound hunting for leopards, Gerard explained, is a very dangerous proposition. Unlike American cougars, which often tree when pursued by hounds, leopards will usually bay. In treeless areas like the Khomas, the cat would likely stand and fight in the rocks and canyons. Leopards vary greatly in their response to hounds and the sight of approaching hunters. Some cats will charge hunters on sight, sending the yammering dogs scurrying in all directions with a furious charge that is as likely as not to result in someone being seriously injured or killed. Unlike hunting out of a blind, where the cat is usually caught unawares by the waiting hunters, bringing a leopard to bay with hounds means that the cat will already be agitated and boiling for a fight.

As the heat of late afternoon faded into night, Gerard and his client sat outside on the veranda and ate their dinner of oryx filets in the approaching darkness. The last traces of purple streamed across the western horizon like a dim aurora burning at the edge of the earth, and stars glimmering like ice crystals hung above the cold desert sky. The quadrangle of the Southern Cross appeared, a lopsided compass needle pointing southward, among the scattered desert stars. Soon the moon rose over the peaks and the rocky slopes of the Khomas Hochland were awash in a milky hue.

Gerard was pushing the last of his oryx filet across the plate with his fork when he heard a series of raspy coughs echoing up through the bare rocks from the canyon below. The sound continued for several seconds, a string of guttural growls that came in rapid succession. As quickly as the growls started, they abruptly stopped, and the night air was left to absorb the echoes.

"Is that the leopard?" Gerard's client asked.

"Yes." Gerard nodded in the half-dark of the veranda and took the last bite of oryx. "That's him."

Sometime later the cat started again, this time calling from farther down the canyon so that the sound echoed over the rock walls and inky black slides. Then the leopard was gone.

It was quite an exciting end to the day. The dishes were done and Gerard bid his client goodnight, both of them heading for bed to dream about the hunt for the big leopard that was at that very moment prowling the dimly lit canyons of the Khomas just below the ridge where they slept.

Wake-up was at four in the morning. The stars that had been dim the night before were a glistening spray of brilliant blue white, and moonlight covered the landscape with light so pure white that it was possible to read a newspaper. The men loaded their gear into the truck, and Gerard cranked the engine until it started and set out with his client into the still night.

The hunters were to meet Roy Sparks and his dog handlers at a nearby ranch. Despite the proximity of the property, it would take the men almost two hours to reach their rendezvous point because of the rough, sandy roads and a series of gates that divided the cattle ranch into different pastures. Each of the gates had to be opened and closed manually, a process that took a great deal of time. With each stop, the cold night air swept into the cab of the pickup.

An hour into the drive, Gerard looked over at his client, who was sitting very still and looking thoughtfully into the darkness. On a long stretch of empty road Gerard suddenly let out a roar that sent his client up against the door. The client turned to Gerard with wide eyes, perhaps thinking his otherwise mentally sound PH had mixed alcohol with his malaria prophylaxis and suffered a bad reaction.

"Did you say your prayers?" Gerard asked.

His client looked back out the window, then turned and spoke slowly. "Yes, I did."

"Good, my friend," Gerard said and smiled, slowing to avoid hitting a hare that scuttled along the right edge of the roadway. "It's always good to say your prayers before a leopard hunt."

As they neared the ranch headquarters, Gerard saw the shining silver reflection of eyes to the left of the vehicle. A dozen long-eared, humpbacked cattle stood behind thin steel wires, their eyes reflecting white as the headlights caught them. As the men slowed to open the gate, a couple of the cattle lumbered off into the thorns while others stood transfixed and stupid in the lights as the truck pulled through. The eastern sky was softening and the rolling plains took shape in the dull light of false dawn. As morning broke, they arrived at the ranch where Roy and his handlers were waiting.

Roy's collection of hounds was a mixed menagerie of foxhound and blue-tick crosses, native mixed-breeds, and even a lone Jack Russell terrier named Oscar. When Gerard and his client arrived, Roy's handlers let some of the dogs out to stretch. Oscar leaped down and ran around the men's legs, shaking with excitement and looking each man over with his black button eyes before running into the gray bush. Upon Oscar's return, the men set out for the riverbed in search of the leopard's tracks.

The spoor of the big male leopard. (Photo courtesy of Gerard Erasmus)

By the time the sun was up, the men had traveled over most of the riverbeds that could be easily accessed on the ranch and had seen no sign of the cat. Based on its movements the night before, it seemed almost certain that the cat had come this way, but not one single fresh track could be found along the miles of sandy riverbed that cut down the canyon between two high hills. Gerard found it hard to believe that the cat had not moved down into the part of the ranch where water and food were available; if the cat had come down from the hills into the ranch country it was almost certain to have traveled along the riverbeds.

It was approaching ten o'clock and the sun was high over the distant hilltops. The dogs had stopped whining in the truck and now lay scattered, their legs and tails and long, pendulous ears lopped one on top of the other as they dozed in the midmorning sun. Even Oscar, once dauntless in his desire to take on a leopard, stretched out and blinked away the light that filtered into the truck as though he had abandoned any hope of finding game and had settled for spending the day drifting in and out of sleep as the truck jolted over the sand.

Just after ten, the men stopped. The hounds stood up and wagged tentative tails while the men gathered on the sand and discussed what could be done. Their options were few. Soon the desert sun would dry out any spoor and all hope of tracking the leopard that day would be lost in the dust and dry haze of the afternoon. With only a few hours of good scent remaining, the men decided to try one last location, a patch of very thick cover high in the hills that the owner of the farm had not ventured into in years. It made sense that a leopard, particularly an old cattle killer such as the one they were hunting, would disappear into such a maze of thorn and shadows to avoid the heat of midday and the wrath of the farmer who had lost dozens of cattle to the cat.

The area was an incredibly thick plot of land high on a hillside. The only way that the men could pass through it was to walk in single file along the game trails cut by generations of animals traveling along the same routes from feeding areas to bedding and water. It was on one of these trails that the men found the track of the old tom leopard. The

The end of the race. The big male leopard nearly eluded the hunters. (Photo courtesy of Gerard Erasmus)

cat had spent the night with a female high in the rocky thorn country. That was why they had heard the cat roaring the night before. Now the male had followed the female high up into the thick cover on the ridge where they would likely wait out the heat of midday.

Roy got word back to his men to get the hounds. Gerard's client pulled his rifle, a .30-06 bolt action, from its case and loaded the magazine while Gerard fed 400-grain slugs into the belly of his Benelli shotgun. The short-barrel 12-gauge was ideal for backing clients at close range when the shots were likely to be fast and the shooting intense. Gerard pressed the action release and the Benelli slammed shut with a mechanical slap, feeding one of the slugs into the chamber. They were off.

Seven hounds were allowed to leap down out of the truck, and the handler leashed them together. Tumbling and straining at the ends of their leads, the hounds pulled against the handler, who periodically pulled them back and cursed at them under his breath in Afrikaans. Like a many-headed Cerberus, the dogs pulled forward as one, their long ears catching in the thorns as they drove forward into the bush, their long tails batting against one another as they strained to start the chase.

The men stood on the edge of the brush and watched the long-legged, lanky hounds cutting back and forth over the track. With each fresh muzzle full of scent, the dogs grew more excited, working their way up the ridge until one opened up on the track and filled the quiet canyon with a deep bawl that echoed down the rocks. Soon the others joined in, and together the pack picked up speed, crying out in a half-dozen voices as they headed up through the brush and rocks. Soon the pack crested the ridge and disappeared over the opposite side.

With his client close beside him, Gerard switched the shotgun to his other hand and they started up the ridge, listening to the furious cries of the hounds that were coursing the leopard down the opposite canyon. Roy, who had the other eight dogs with him, traveled with the men up over the ridge and was all set to turn the other dogs loose when a commotion broke out among the dogs and the handler in the canyon below. The hot, rapid barks of pursuit had changed in an instant to terrified howls and the handler shouted from the rocks below. The cat had doubled back on its own trail and had run headlong through the pack, scattering its pursuers as it rushed through their ranks with a thunderous roar.

The remaining members of the pack were turned loose and the chase boiled down into the shadowy belly of the canyon, where all that could be heard were the frantic howls of the dogs and the occasional roar or growl from the cat. Gerard pulled his client forward among the big rocks that lined the canyon floor. The cat could be hiding in any thicket or rockslide. It could also, as they had just seen, change direction and plow through the hunters once again. Perhaps the next time the cat rushed its pursuers, it would not be content to simply part them and move on.

It was impossible to pinpoint exactly where the sounds came from in the echoing melee among the rocks. Gerard fanned the Benelli and remained ready to take a snap shot in case the leopard decided to charge the men on sight. There were grunts mixed with the cacophony of the baying dogs. A whimper filled the air and then the faint sound was lost in the increasing chorus of the dogs as they fought the leopard in the sandy earth just below the hunters.

"There he is!" Gerard shouted, and pulled his client forward into position.

The cat had leaped up onto a flat rock and stood looking down at the dogs, its huge head cocked back, fangs out. Every few seconds the cat would give a coughing roar and rush at the dogs, swiping at them with its wide paw and slashing at the air with its deadly white claws. At this, the dogs would fall back in a tumbling, bawling mass, only to gather their ranks and push back up toward the rock. During one rush, the cat disappeared from sight and there was an awful howling and the snap of teeth. As the cat reappeared on the large rock, the hounds pressed forward, bawling with a new fury.

Gerard instructed his client to shoot the cat and do it quickly before the leopard slipped away from the pack or caught another of the dogs with a raking slash of its paw. At seventy-five yards his client took a rest on a rock, found the cat in the scope, and tried to center the cross hairs on the rapidly moving target. With eyes wide and hateful, the leopard made another rush at the pack, which scattered into the shadows and thorns around the base of the rock. Then the cat sat back on the rock and settled on its haunches, giving Gerard's client a brief moment to settle the cross hairs, catch his breath, and press the trigger.

The shot echoed down the rocky walls of the canyon, a terrific boom that split the air and was swallowed up by the resurrected voices of the dogs as they pressed in again toward the dead leopard, which now lay stretched out at full length on the rock. Even after the cat's death, the dogs refused to come closer than the base of the rock.

Gerard could not believe the size of the leopard. He and his client approached the flat-topped stone slowly, with Gerard holding the bead of the Benelli in the center of the cat's chest as he waited for any sign of life. There was none. The 165-grain softpoint had done its job, and the cat was stone dead by the time the men reached it.

They found that one of the dogs in the pack had met an unfortunate end during the moments before Gerard and his client got into position to kill the cat. The others were leashed and held back as the men looked over the old cattle killer. Its shoulders and legs were thick and muscled, and its face was a network of glossy purple scars from a lifetime spent fighting other leopards in the dark canyons of the Khomas Hochland. The leopard had made a fine living stealing calves and killing antelope in the hills. Its belly hung low and its neck was a thick, knotted mass of muscle that bulged against the back of its skull. In Afrikaans, the term *groot kop* means "big head," and this leopard now had a new name. For recordkeeping purposes, cats are gauged by the measurements of their skulls. The big leopard of the Khomas proved to be a *groot kop* indeed, with a skull measuring 18¾ inches, placing the cat among the largest ever taken in Namibia.

After the 2009 closure of leopard hunting with hounds, stories like this one are a thing of the past . . . at least for now. For those hunters who took part in these leopard hunts, however, the memory of the chase and that first close encounter with a furious cat will always be foremost in their minds. There are few things in life that can compare to looking into the eyes of a deadly cat at point-blank range.

CHAPTER 5

The Balyerwa Bull

Professional hunter: Karl Stumpfe
Location: Caprivi

Karl Stumpfe of Ndumo Safaris stood over the tracks and looked out toward the island of land perched among the floodwater channels of the Kwando River. Heavy rains in the early months of 2009 had caused the vegetation in the Caprivi Strip to grow to record heights. The savanna, normally a green, rolling grassland dotted with patches of thorn and trees, had been turned into a series of scattered islands rising from the brown floodwater. The game in the region, particularly elephants, flourished with the abundant growth. Since the elephants could cross the channels from island to island swiftly and easily, they enjoyed a bounty during the period of heavy flooding that year.

For elephant hunters, however, the floods meant difficult hunting. The trackers had to try to follow the spoor of the elephant herds as they moved from island to island, and the hunting party had to cross the chest-deep channels with guns held high overhead, always wondering if a stray hippo or crocodile had found its way into the pools from the main channel of the Kwando.

The tracks of the trio of elephant bulls Karl was following with his client, John Philip Thoreson, led up to the edge of the swollen water and vanished into the current. It was clear that the narrow island across the channel was where the elephant bulls had headed. Whether or not they were still there was yet to be seen. Karl moved into the water first, the cool breath of the moving current rising along his ankles and calves as he forded the channel just as the elephants had done. Behind him came his client; Stumpfe's tracker, Derek; and finally the game scout, Justus. They made their way across the flooded channel, feeling the invisible touch of reeds and papyrus brushing against their legs in the brown water below. The cold water rose up to the men's chests as they crossed the channel, their rifles held high, and emerged on the far bank. They stood for a moment as shimmering drops of water fell

Crossing the flooded channels of the Kwando River in search of elephant. (Photo courtesy of Karl Stumpfe/Ndumo Safaris)

from their wet clothes, looking down at the dinner-plate-size tracks of the elephants.

The spoor led from the reeds into the forest of tangled green Combretum and thorns that covered the island. Still untouched by the highest of the floodwaters, the game trails on the interior portion of the island were dry and hard-packed from the weight of animals that had passed along these narrow corridors for generations. The elephant spoor was lost on this hard, gray ground, but the hunters saw evidence that the bulls had passed this way: the splintered white shards of a broken limb, a torn and half-eaten branch lying on the trail.

Karl slowed the men and they listened for the sounds of the elephants ahead. Nothing. The only sound was the slight stirring of the breeze through the Combretum bush, and the only movement was the slight weaving of darkness and light as the shadows of limbs swayed on the hard-packed earth ahead. In the dark, tangled forest, Karl looked through the interwoven green limbs for any sign of the bulls. Chances were that the men would not see the elephants in this green morass until they were all but on top of them.

A hundred yards deeper into the trees, Karl saw a piece of an elephant through a narrow tunnel in the green foliage. It was impossible to say what portion of the elephant's anatomy he was looking at, and he could not know which of the three bulls it was. The men inched closer, hoping for a better look to determine which of the three bulls had the best ivory. Karl maneuvered through the dense growth, avoiding the dry sticks on the ground and hoping the wet squish of his boots would not alert the elephants as he duck-walked forward and sideways through the bush toward the feeding elephants.

After some time, Karl managed to assess the ivory and decided that the bull closest to the men was most likely the one they wanted. He brought his client close to him and they waited as the elephant moved through the shadows ahead, appearing in patches of black and gray as it passed from sun to shade while feeding.

"I'd really like to have a look at that right-side ivory once more," Karl said quietly.

Trying to get a clear view of anything in the forest was going to be difficult, especially since the bulls had turned and were moving away from the men. Karl and John Philip moved forward slowly, trying to avoid the dry, brown leaves scattered across the hard-packed trail, which was as solid as a New York sidewalk. But the bulls would not cooperate. They continued to move away, moving left and right ahead of the men in the forest. Finally Karl and John Philip cut into the thicket in an attempt to get a last look at the ivory to ensure it was as good as they hoped.

The men were off to the left of the trail and moving through the dense cover behind the elephants when the bull they were following suddenly turned and raised its great head. The bull's thick, wrinkled trunk rose up, and its wide ears opened. Through the cover, Karl could see the tattered edges of the elephant's ears and its swaying trunk. The great head moved left and right, testing the wind and listening intently, while Karl and John Philip stood still, waiting for a chance at the huge tusker.

Something had alerted the bull. Perhaps it had heard the dry, sharp snap of a branch underfoot or caught the scent of man on a swirling wind. Perhaps it had even sensed the vibrations of the men walking. Whatever it was that had alerted the bull did not matter much. Soon it and the others would be gone.

"You've got to try to shoot," Karl said in a forced, dry whisper as the men stood and leveled their rifles.

It was not easy to see the bull's vitals through the wall of thorn, but Karl found his mark over the iron sights of his .450 Rigby Rimless rifle. He waited for John Philip's shot, ready to deliver an instant backup shot as his client had requested.

From his right, Karl felt the blast of his client's rifle, and almost before he could see the impact of the shot striking the bull's shoulder, he fired his own gun. The five-hundred-grain solid hit with a tremendous *whump* against the bull's shoulder and raised a cloud of dust. The elephant spun, its head high, trumpeting as it ran a few steps toward the other bulls before collapsing in the Combretum thicket, dead before it hit the ground.

There was no time for congratulations or celebration after the bull went down. The elephant's two companions came thundering back down the hard-packed game trail toward them, charging through the trees and flattening the dense green bushes that grew alongside the path. Karl grabbed his client and together they moved away from the trail, hoping that the bulls would pass by. Karl thought about his tracker, Derek, and Justus, the game scout, and hoped that the two men would be able to avoid the oncoming elephants.

The rushing elephants were about to pass Karl and John Philip when the closest bull suddenly changed direction and came barreling through the green growth toward Karl. With the bull running directly

Karl and his client with the bull that Karl killed in defense of himself and his client. (Photo courtesy of Karl Stumpfe)

perpendicular to its original path, there was little question that the elephant had either seen or smelled Karl and his client and was coming for them. Karl shouted and waved his rifle, hoping that the elephant could be bluffed. It became instantly apparent, though, that the bull steamrolling its way toward the men was not going to be turned. It would have to be stopped. Karl swung the rifle up to his shoulder, found the bull's head over the irons, aimed just above the eyes, and pressed the trigger.

At the shot, the bull was almost towering over the men. The flat, hard slap of the bullet resounded over the crash of the rifle and the trumpet of the elephant. In an instant, the bull dropped down into the brush, clearing a great swath in the heavy Combretum. In the sudden stillness, the sun shone down through the canopy and onto the dead bull, which lay flat on its belly not more than a couple of yards away from Karl.

Karl ejected the spent round and chambered a fresh cartridge as he ran almost within touching distance of the dead bull to an open place where he could see the third elephant rushing headlong through the forest, its retreat echoing with the sharp cracks of limbs and a heavy shuffling sound. Karl's leg became tangled in a twisted limb and he went down hard, listening to the shouts of his men from across the forest and the shuffling and trumpeting of the elephant as it made its way back toward the river.

Karl was up in an instant and checked on his client. John Philip was fine, although somewhat pale, as could be expected given the circumstances. Karl then went back to the trail and followed the fleeing elephant's tracks back toward where he had last seen the tracker and game scout. The elephant was long gone, but there were no signs of Derek and Justus. They were not where Karl had last seen them and there was no sign of them in the surrounding bush. They hadn't been ground into the dirt, at least that Karl could see. Where could they have gone?

Derek was the first to return to the scene. As the bull thundered toward him, he saw that his only option was to dive through the vegetation and jump into the river. Soaked and exhausted, he said that Justus had taken flight in the opposite direction when the bull came, and since then Derek had seen no sign of him. Shortly thereafter, the game scout came out of the bush, exasperated and shirtless. He explained that when the bull had come, he had taken flight through the thorns, and, when his shirt caught on the arms of a thornbush, he slipped out of it and ran bare-chested through the forest until the crashing and trumpeting had subsided. Somehow, miraculously, no one had been hurt in the melee.

John Philip's bull was an excellent trophy with beautiful ivory. The old bull had tusks that were thinner and longer than most of the other bulls in the region; it looked more like an East African elephant than a Caprivi bull.

After a successful hunt in the Caprivi. (Photo courtesy of Karl Stumpfe)

The immediate threat had passed, but Karl had a serious legal matter to deal with. Even though the second bull was killed in self-defense and to protect his client, Karl had nevertheless killed an elephant bull for which he did not have a license. The only recourse was to be honest and straightforward in his report to the Namibian government. Karl made detailed drawings of the scene and gave his testimony to the government along with the names of all the witnesses present. After reviewing the facts of the case, the Namibian government found that Karl had acted in the best interests of his client; if he had not taken the action he did, his client would very likely have been killed. The second bull was declared a problem animal, and Karl was found innocent of any wrongdoing.

An elephant at close range peers through the dense green cover of Namibia's Caprivi Strip. (Photo courtesy of Jacques Strauss)

Like many such incidents, it had happened in an instant, a breathless moment that forced a professional hunter to stand his ground and act in the best interests of himself, his team, and his client. A minor slip-up in such a situation might spell death for those relying on him. Karl had passed the ultimate test.

CHAPTER 6

Slang!

Professional hunter: Bijorn le Roux
Location: Etosha Conservancy

It was midwinter in the Etosha Conservancy in northwestern Namibia. Bijorn le Roux, a professional hunter with Mashete Safaris, was leading his German client out to an elevated blind near a water hole on the third day of the safari. The German wanted a good warthog boar and Bijorn knew of an old warthog male with wide, deeply curled ivory that frequented the pan. Little did Bijorn know that a few hours later he would be trapped with one of Africa's deadliest creatures.

The blind was made of wide boards separated by narrow gaps for ventilation with a piece of corrugated steel on top to reflect sunlight and repel rain. It was positioned on four poles fifteen feet tall and ten inches in diameter set deep in the rocky soil, and it offered a perfect vantage point to view the muddy water hole the big warthog had been frequenting. In the still, gray morning, the surface of the water appeared olive-green, and turtledoves moved in small circles, stirring dust at the water's edge.

Bijorn sat in the corner of the blind farthest from the entry ladder and the German client sat next to him. Jeremiah, a Damara man in his midthirties and Mashete's lead tracker, sat closest to the door. Jeremiah was a tall, thin man with sharp, chocolate-colored eyes and a sun-weathered face the color of a kudu's horn.

When the men were settled on the narrow bench, Jeremiah pulled a pinch of dry tobacco from the pouch in his heavy coat and a thin sheet of newspaper from another pocket. In the quiet of first light, Jeremiah slowly and carefully rolled the tobacco into the newsprint, then struck a match and lit the narrow tip of the homemade cigarette. The German client leaned his rifle against the front of the blind and settled down between his PH and tracker. As the sun rose and warmed the blind, the men sat silently side-by-side on the narrow seat, watching as the doves flew up into the trees and were replaced on the water's edge by a flock

Professional hunter Bijorn le Roux of Mashete Safaris hunting in the Etosha Conservancy. (Photo courtesy of Benjamin Gettinger)

of helmeted guinea fowls that emerged from the trees and trotted out into the open space by the pan.

Hours passed and the sun rose over the tops of the scattered thorn trees. The chill of morning was replaced by the dry heat of a Namibian winter day. The guineas finished their drink and scuttled in the dirt around the water hole, scratching for bugs and chasing each other over the hard-packed earth at the edge of the thorn thicket. The morning silence was broken with the constant yammering of the guineas. A flock of brilliant blue starlings lit on the edge of the water, taking rapid drinks in succession as they watched for predators. Both the guineas and the starlings scattered as the shadow of a passing hawk crossed the dry earth in front of the blind. The guineas, looking like a flock of overweight women in polka-dotted hoop dresses, scurried toward the protection of the devil thorns. As the birds ran, the men listened to their rattling calls fade into the shadows of the thorns.

Other game came to the water hole. A small herd of kudu cows and calves appeared about nine o'clock, moving with profound caution from the trees into the open. After the kudus left, a warthog sow and three small piglets came down, drinking and wallowing before turning and running back into the cover that surrounded the water, their tufted tails pointing up in an attitude of imminent doom. The boar, however, did not show itself.

As the sun warmed the metal roof, the scratchy footsteps of lizards could be heard on the corrugated roof of the blind. The constant clatter was unnerving at first, but after the hunters had spent several hours in the high seat, the scratch of the lizards on the roof became as much a part of the daily chatter of the African bush as the tinny call of the guineas or the coo of the doves in the surrounding treetops.

On that day, like any other in that particular blind, the tinny scratch of lizard claws on the metal roof began as soon as the sun was up, for that was when the small dark lizards that lived in the surrounding acacias climbed onto the roof to warm their bodies. From inside the blind, it was possible to trace their movements by listening to the progress of their tiny feet over the artificial hills and valleys of the metal roof. Sometimes a lizard would travel all the way to the edge of the metal and sit on one of the boards on the side of the blind, visible to the men inside. These lizards provided entertainment for the long, quiet periods when no game was present at the water hole. The dust-

Climbing into an elevated blind. Little did the hunters know that a deadly serpent would surprise them not once but twice that day. (Photo courtesy of Benjamin Gettinger)

colored reptiles could be heard constantly shuffling overhead like assembly-line employees assuming their positions at the beginning of the workday. Then, suddenly, the sound of their movements stopped altogether.

The German client paid no attention to the clamor of the lizards or to the sudden silence. Bijorn and Jeremiah, both bush-savvy, immediately took note of the sudden departure of the lizards from the rooftop. Perhaps, Bijorn thought, there was another predatory bird passing in the air overhead. But he saw no shadow tracing its way over the ground. Finally, Bijorn decided that the lizards had warmed themselves and had simply found other ways to entertain themselves rather than chasing one another over the roof of the blind.

Then came a steady rasping against the metal roof that sounded as though a heavy, fibrous rope was being dragged over the corrugated panels. Bijorn turned to Jeremiah and they looked at one another as the sinister sound echoed in the small blind. The client continued to watch for warthogs, oblivious to the increasingly stern glances being passed between PH and tracker and the growing tension they shared regarding this new, awful sound from the metal sheets overhead.

The sound came again, a cold, steady tugging across the length of the metal roof; the sound was frighteningly alive, as though the men could hear muscles working behind the whine of the metal. Then the sound stopped. Bijorn felt a moment's panic and knew his worst fears were realized. There was a snake on the roof just above them.

Bijorn decided that he had better send Jeremiah out of the blind to determine the size and the species of the serpent that rested just inches above their heads. The tracker obliged, despite his lifelong fear of snakes. Jeremiah slowly rose from the wooden bench, leaned out the doorway, and turned to look at the rooftop. Long seconds passed as Jeremiah studied the situation. Finally, he sat back down in the blind, doing his best to maintain his composure.

"*Slang,*" he said, almost casually. Snake. Bijorn asked in Afrikaans what type of snake it was.

"Boomslang," Jeremiah said. The boomslang is a deadly, rear-fanged tree snake that can kill a man with a single bite.

Bijorn tensed. Jeremiah continued in Afrikaans so that the client would not understand. He said a very large boomslang had crawled into the blind from a nearby tree. It was not on the roof, as expected, but had found its way under the corrugated metal and was lying in the thin space between the wooden boards and the metal. The scraping sound was a result of the snake's back, not its belly, sliding against the roof metal. The only thing separating the snake from the hunters was a thin layer of cracked wooden planks.

That was enough for Bijorn. He didn't want to put his client in danger with a very venomous snake at such close quarters. He started to ask his client to step out of the blind when he suddenly saw the snake's spear-shaped head and part of its body extending from the back wall into the blind at cheek level. Bijorn froze and watched the snake, its dull brown head held steady as its tongue flickered in the cold morning air. If the snake decided to strike from its position against the back wall, it would surely bite one of the men in the face or neck.

Bijorn ordered Jeremiah and the client to slowly and steadily move to the door and climb out of the blind. They did as Bijorn asked, moving toward the open doorway on the left of the blind without questioning the PH. Bijorn watched the snake, its round, cold eyes unblinking behind the glossy tongue that flitted in and out of the awful mouth that housed the short, deadly fangs. When the client moved, Bijorn saw the snake turn toward the man, its head cocked to the left and a U-shaped curl in its neck as if preparing to strike. It would have been impossible for the snake to reach either the German or Jeremiah with only a small portion of its body within the blind. The snake would have to come farther in before it could bite either one, and Bijorn breathed a sigh of relief when the client's head finally disappeared down the ladder and out of sight.

With the client and Jeremiah on the ground, Bijorn felt a great relief that he had gotten them out safely. He had not, however, expected to find

The deadly boomslang, or tree snake, is arboreal and can climb quite well. This rear-fanged snake can administer a deadly bite, and being cornered by one in the confines of a blind is a nightmare. (Photo courtesy of Jofie Lamprecht)

himself trapped by the snake. But ensnared he was, holding his breath while pinned against the wall not far from the deadly boomslang's scaly body that was extending two feet into the blind. Had he been prone to suicidal fancies, Bijorn could have reached out and touched the snake's narrow head.

He began to look around the blind, hoping to find something to defend himself with if the snake became agitated. Bijorn needed to do something and quickly since the snake's body seemed to be sprouting out of the roof of the blind. He watched as the dull brown body extended steadily from the space overhead.

Bijorn found a cast-off wooden plank on the floor with a rusted nail sticking through it. He picked it up slowly, then turned his attention back to the snake, which was easing farther and farther into the blind. Bijorn's mind raced as he watched the snake, knowing full well that it might strike him at any moment if he moved. He tried hard not to think about the toxic cocktail of venom inside the snake's mouth and the deadly efficiency with which it would work on his body.

Time was running out. The boomslang was now dangerously close. Knowing he had only one chance to survive, Bijorn furiously swung the wooden plank down at an angle. The force of the blow drove the snake's head back against the wall, trapping the serpent. Enraged, the snake lashed out in a fury, biting blindly at Bijorn and curling its long body around the plank. By an incredible stroke of luck, Bijorn had driven the point of the rusted nail into the snake's body and had pinned the boomslang to the wall. This kept the furious snake from reaching Bijorn even though it launched a series of vigorous, deadly strikes. With the boomslang pinned against the wall, Bijorn had time to bolt through the opening of the blind and leap down the wooden ladder to safety.

Bijorn landed in the sand and turned around to look back up into the blind. The snake was still thrashing and writhing; the men could see the boomslang's dark shadow slashing across the golden glow of the morning sun reflecting off the back of the blind. Finally there was a great clatter of wood hitting wood—the rattle of the loosened wooden plank hitting the floor as the enraged snake finally managed to free itself. The boomslang fell in a thrashing ball onto the floor of the blind and then tumbled out the doorway over the ladder, almost landing on the hunters as they scrambled back away from the blind. The snake's long coils landed with a meaty thump on the sand and raised a cloud of shimmering silver dust. Finally freed from the nail and thoroughly infuriated, the snake hissed and struck wildly as it slithered back into heavy cover and disappeared out of sight.

The men did a quick check for snakebites and found that, miraculously, all of them had escaped the blind unbitten. Bijorn's client seemed oblivious to the seriousness of the encounter; he appeared more than a little annoyed at being interrupted during his morning hunt.

After the punctured snake vanished into the long grass and all was quiet again at the water hole, the men set out to check the perimeter of the tree. There was no sign of the snake except the distinct S-shaped spoor left behind in the sand where it had escaped after the fall. Slowly, the men climbed back up the ladder, looking carefully into the blind for any sign of the snake before entering the metal box that had almost served as their coffin. Jeremiah and Bijorn looked down from the blind to check the surrounding cover quite often, but they did not imagine the snake would return after the rough handling it had received during its last trip into the blind.

But the boomslang did return. Bijorn glanced out the narrow window and saw the snake once again slithering up through the branches, picking its way from one limb to the next in a steady and deliberate path back toward the blind. At first Bijorn could not believe that this was the same snake, but the nail hole in its side indicated that it was, in fact, the same reptile they had dealt with only moments earlier.

The hunters piled furiously out of the blind and scrambled down the ladder, cursing at the lithe snake that seemed bent on evicting the men once and for all from its adopted home. This time Bijorn decided to make sure of the snake's condition before they returned to the blind. Jeremiah found a wrist-thick branch on the ground and broke it into two unequal-length pieces. Taking the shorter section, Jeremiah circled the base of the tree. He studied the loops of the snake's long body for a moment. Gauging the angle, Jeremiah flung the short stick into the tree, spinning it end-over-end like a tomahawk. It struck the snake midbody and brought it to the ground with a thump. Before the snake could gather itself to strike, Jeremiah was on it with the larger portion of the branch, striking two quick blows to the snake's head. That ended the fight.

Even though the boomslang was dead, none of the men cared to venture back into the blind that day, so they decided to head back to camp without their warthog. Perhaps they would try again the following morning.

Not long after the incident with the boomslang, Bijorn and Jeremiah were riding in the back of an open hunting car when Jeremiah bailed out of the bed with a scream and shouted, "*Slang!*" Bijorn turned to see the cold, gray gaze of a large black mamba that had reared itself to the height of the truck bed as they passed. Most likely it had been hunting in the brush near the road and the noise of the truck had upset it. Bijorn said the snake did one heck of a job of upsetting him as well.

CHAPTER 7

The Ten-Mile Bull

Professional hunter: Hannes du Plessis
Location: Central Highlands

By the time professional hunter Hannes du Plessis and his clients, Robert Bernardi and Al Strup, caught up with the hartebeest bull, darkness was closing in. It was March of 2007, still early in the hunting season, and Hannes's Bergzicht hunting farm was still green from the last heavy rains. As the light faded, Hannes examined the bull, which stood in a narrow patch of open ground between two patches of thorn. The hartebeest's bell-shaped horns were high and heavy, and Hannes knew from the thickness of its shoulders and its sagging belly that this was an old hartebeest. The bull had stopped not far from the boundary fence that separated Bergzicht from a neighboring farm. It now stood stock-still, giving the hunting party one long, last look as it readied itself to bound into cover in search of the cows that were just ahead. Without a doubt, the hartebeest was a mature bull and a fine trophy, but Al would have to act fast.

Hannes turned to Al and told him that if he wanted a hartebeest bull, now was the time. Al stepped down from the car and made his way through the bush toward Hannes. When he located the bull, Al rested his rifle on a branch and centered the cross hairs on the bull's broad, dark chest. The .375 Remington Ultra Magnum bellowed, rising up off the wooden branch with a thunderous jolt. The 260-grain Nosler Accubond struck the bull just behind the foreleg with a thump that could be heard over the crash of the rifle. At the shot the hartebeest stopped, then gathered itself and started across the plains in a rocking gallop that carried it toward the fence. Almost without breaking stride, the bull dropped and slid under the strands of wire, rose, and resumed its full gallop before Al's rifle cracked a second time and the bull lurched, cantering off into the coming darkness.

They had to wait. Pushing the wounded bull now meant the possibility of spooking the animal and prolonging the search. If the

African plains game can be difficult to bring down, as evidenced by the hartebeest that Hannes du Plessis and his client trailed for miles after the shot. (Photo by Jacques Strauss)

hunters stumbled upon the wounded bull even in its last moments, it was possible that the hartebeest would spook and run for miles in the darkness. Like most African plains game, the hartebeest has a well-deserved reputation for resilience unmatched by game animals anywhere else in the world. Even a chest shot from a big rifle such as the .375 might not put the bull down immediately, and as the distance between hunter and quarry lengthened, so did the chances of losing the bull. There was nothing to do now but wait for the hartebeest to stiffen up and hope to find it in the morning before the jackals and hyenas did.

As the last daylight faded and the chill of night came on, the men headed back to the truck. Al placed his rifle back in the rack and climbed aboard as the motor started and the dim yellow headlights illuminated the sandy road that would lead the men back to the lodge. It was a cold ride.

Back at camp, the men ate a solemn dinner. Al worried that his shots had not been good, but Hannes assured him that the bull would probably expire and said that at first light they would set out. In the light of day the odds would be on the side of the hunters, especially the eagle-eyed trackers employed by Bergzicht. Hannes was confident that in the morning when the men took up the track they would find the two bullets Al had fired had slowed the bull's progress. As dinner ended and the fire was stoked, the men sat under a ceiling of stars that stretched like a great, shimmering belt across the desert sky, illuminating the plains. Al and Hannes watched as the sweet mopane-wood fire slowly simmered and died in the moonlight.

Daylight brought with it great hope and expectation as the men loaded their gear into the hunting truck. It was autumn in the southern hemisphere, and the mornings were not yet as cold as they would be in a few months. As the sun broke over the distant yellow hills, Hannes reassured his client that they would get the bull. He was sure that both of Al's shots had connected and that the bull would have died or at least slowed down during the night.

Four of Hannes's best trackers stood around the truck talking quietly as the sun rose and cast long shadows across the sandy parking lot beside the lodge. After breakfast and good-byes to the lodge staff, Al, Hannes, and Al's hunting companion, Bob, got into the cab of the truck, and the solemn, businesslike trackers climbed into the back. By the time the first warm wind blew across the plains, the men were already cutting a path through the green-and-yellow grass toward the place where they had last seen the bull.

The fact that the bull had slipped under the boundary fence was not a problem. Bergzicht Ranch covered almost 40,000 hectares, or 60,000 acres. It belonged to a communal conservancy made up of a number of adjoining farms, totaling almost half a million acres of hunting land. The farm where the bull had escaped onto was part of the conservancy, and little more than a smile and a wave were needed to gain the hunters access to the place where the hartebeest had escaped through the boundary fence.

In the morning light, the team of trackers quickly found the bull's trail. The heart-shaped tracks led into the thornscrub, spaced well apart for the first hundred yards as the bull ran, and then growing closer together as the hartebeest slowed from the impact of the shot. Round, glossy splotches of blood, now dull and dry in the morning sun, had scattered along both sides of the track as the bull made its way through the tangles of thorn.

Throughout the morning and into the heat of midday, the men followed, the trackers often stopping and talking quietly among themselves, the hunters behind them. On more than one occasion, the track was lost in a patch of grass or on hard earth and the trackers had to work to unravel the trail, their dark skin becoming glossy with sweat as the sun rose higher.

Hours passed and the men continued on, walking so far from the truck that they had to stop and turn back at one point to regain their bearings. Al had carried his nine-pound .375 for miles through the heat and was looking more and more worried. The hartebeest continued through the scrubby green cover, following an unknown compass bearing over a series of interwoven game trails that led across dry riverbeds, plains, and through thorn forests. The blood trail thinned, too. Hannes had noticed that, but he did not mention it to his client.

All of Africa's game have a reputation for a tenacious refusal to die, even when shot well. Hartebeests are among Africa's elite game animals, and they often will not drop even when shot multiple times with magnum rifles. This bull, true to the nature of the species, kept moving steadily away from the place where it had been shot, and by afternoon it appeared that the men might not find it.

Then, just as the reality of the situation began to sink in, one of the trackers lowered himself and pointed toward a thornbush a hundred yards ahead. There, silhouetted in the shadows of the thorny branches, they saw the outline of the bull. The hartebeest offered them only a fleeting look before turning and galloping away into the thorns. By the time Al was ready to shoot, the bull was little more than a rusty red form moving quickly through the scattered thorns. There was no chance for a shot.

Many PHs would have turned back at the sight of the bull galloping farther out of reach, and even Hannes might have given up had he not had complete faith in his tracking team. The trackers stood together and watched the bull gallop out of sight, their hands shading their faces from the intense sun as the hartebeest slipped silently into dense cover. When the bull was out of sight, the men continued forward. Sapped and strained as they were, the sight of the hartebeest just out of reach was enough to spur the team back into action, and within minutes the trackers were moving in single file along the narrow sand trail. One of the trackers pointed out to Hannes that the bull had slowed quickly and that it wouldn't be far ahead. This time, the men kept watch over the trail ahead in hopes of catching sight of the bull before it made another run.

Without warning the trackers stopped, lowered themselves slowly, and indicated with silent snaps of their fingers that the bull was there. Hannes grabbed his client and together they moved forward toward an opening in the thorn. Just ahead of them was the bull. It stood quartering away from the men and offered another opportunity for a shot. The big

The ten-mile bull. Persistence paid off when Hannes and his client finally collected this good hartebeest. (Photo courtesy of Hannes du Plessis)

.375 came up into position on the sticks, and at the crack of the rifle, the bull dropped in its tracks.

As a plume of dust rose from beneath the downed bull, the hunters made their way up to their fallen adversary. Its horns were just as impressive as Hannes remembered. That, compounded with the fact that it had absorbed two shots from the .375 and had continued on for many miles, made this bull an exceptional trophy regardless of its record-book score. Since the early morning, the men had covered ten dusty, thorn-tattered miles in their pursuit of the hartebeest bull. Al received handshakes from the trackers and a pat on the back from Hannes as he stood over his trophy. The only question that remained was who would be running back ten miles to fetch the truck.

CHAPTER 8

The Charge

Professional hunter: Cornie Coetzee
Location: Kamanjab

Daylight faded into dusk over the dry sand veld near the town of Kamanjab. The landscape was a patchwork of shadows and sunburned grass. Long, red feathers of sunshine caught the dust that hung in the air as the western horizon shimmered in the fading light, and the leafy, flat-topped water acacias cast speckled shadows on the ground. Without a sound, the big male lion moved through the dry winter grass and acacia trees, powerful muscles rippling beneath its tawny hide as it stopped at the edge of the clearing beside a water hole. The cat paused, surveying the open landscape as the black tuft at the end of its tail flitted left and right. There was an offering beside the water hole—a zebra quarter secured to the base of an acacia tree with a bundle of wire. The cat ignored it. It had eaten its fill, and having spent the afternoon in a mopane thicket, it now worked its way down through the low thorns to the edge of the water hole.

When the lion appeared at the edge of the thicket, doves and guinea fowls scattered from the edge of the water. Baboons stood sentinel in the tallest branches of a distant acacia, moving from one limb to the next and bouncing up and down while they announced the lion's presence with a series of deep screams. The lion ignored this ovation and did not even offer the baboon troop a glance. The cat was not hunting. Instead, it glided effortlessly toward the water hole, and when it reached its murky edge, it lowered itself and drank, lapping the water slowly and deliberately with its back-turned tongue.

Across the water hole, two men sat silent and breathless as the lion appeared at the water's edge. A thin screen of dry, interwoven thorns blocked them from the cat's view. While the lion drank its fill in the fading light, the men in the blind argued without words. The professional hunter, Cornie Coetzee, a veteran with more than thirty years of experience in the safari business, calmed his client and ordered

Cornie Coetzee, one of Namibia's top professional hunters. (Photo courtesy of Elaine Coetzee)

him not to shoot, for the lion presented only an awkward frontal shot. His client indicated that he could take the shot and that he would put the cat down without any worries. Cornie had the final say, and since he was the one who would have to follow the lion through the nest of devil's thorn if his client wounded it, he cast the deciding vote.

The two men watched as the lion crouched by the water, the slurping of its tongue audible across the bare space that separated the cat from the men. Finally the lion stood and stretched in the fading light. It turned away from the men without offering a shot and vanished back into the thicket from which it had emerged.

Daylight faded into night and cold air filled the blind just as the first stars appeared on the far horizon. The cat had made no sound since it departed and the two men sat huddled in the blind listening for any clue to the lion's whereabouts. They heard nothing—only the far-off purr of an owl as the smiling sliver of the quarter moon rose over the hills. The cat was gone. Perhaps a drink was all the lion desired, and now it was back in the tangle of thorns where it had spent the day, slumbering in the blue glow of the moon. Then again, maybe the lion had slipped out of the thorns and was cruising silently along the network of game trails that crossed the darkened thorn forest, looking for a kill.

Later, the men returned to the truck and headed back to the camp of CEC Safaris, a long-established company owned by Cornie and his wife, Elaine. Sitting around the campfire with sweating drinks in their hands, Cornie and his hunting guest shared stories and made plans for the next day. Overhead, the desert sky was clear and frosted with the shimmering blue-white glow of countless stars. When the drinks were empty and the desert air was still, Cornie and his client turned in for the night. They had seen the cat that day and had drunk a toast to that. Tomorrow, though, they would get much closer.

Cornie's safari camp was under a grove of thorn trees in the vast, open plains of northern Namibia. The closest village was Kamanjab, a small, dusty town directly south of Etosha National Park and an hour's drive northwest of Outjo on Highway C40. The village is in one of the wildest and most remote regions of the country, a place where Himba people with their red-painted bodies and long, clumped hair still eke out a living on the dry, thorny plains. There are prides of lions that move in and out of the area, as well as the occasional cat that escapes from the park and moves south into the game-rich plains around Kamanjab. These lions are among the largest in Africa, and they are unpredictable in their behavior and moods. Stumbling upon such a cat in dense cover could spell disaster, especially if the lion was part of a mating pair or if it had just made a kill.

For Cornie, there would be no stumbling upon a cat accidentally. He was an experienced lion hunter and he knew just where the lion would be when the hunters returned to the blind the next morning: It was staying within the confines of the mopane thicket during the day. It was tremendous luck to have a trophy lion in the area, and Cornie had no desire to force the male out of the territory by pressuring it. The men backed out of the blind at midmorning and headed back to camp for lunch and a nap in the shade of a camelthorn tree. When the sun tilted toward the west, Cornie collected his client and they returned to the blind by the water's edge to see if the cat would finally offer them the shot they had been waiting for.

It was not long before the lion reappeared. Once again, the starlings and Cape turtledoves that lined the edge of the water hole burst into the air when the cat materialized suddenly and silently at the edge of the thorns. Once again, the lion scanned the open ground near the water hole before coming out of its thorny lair for a drink. The cat bypassed the bait once more and walked stiff-legged down to the water's edge. It followed the same path it had used the night before, and once again offered only a risky frontal shot.

Cornie held his hand up to signal his client not to shoot. From the corner of his eye Cornie could see the man's wide eyes and white-knuckled grip on the walnut stock of his rifle, and he knew that seeing a big trophy lion two nights in a row without getting a chance for a shot might be more than the man could bear.

Cornie gave the lion another look through the field glasses to confirm what he already knew: This was a big cat. The lion's dark mane covered the top of its shoulders and ran down across the wide, muscular chest. Shining gray scars formed a spider's web across the bridge of the cat's nose. From the lion's sagging belly and swayed back, Cornie could tell it was an old male. The lion lowered its chest toward the murky water and started drinking. Just sixty yards away sat a magnificent trophy—and just the kind of cat Cornie and his client were after. Now all that was left was for the lion to offer the hunters a better chance for a shot.

The blind erupted with the roar of a rifle shot. Cornie's client had given in to the temptation to shoot, despite Cornie's insistence that he not do so because of the poor angle the lion presented. The cat rose up and roared, thrashed its tail, struck with its forepaws, and reared again before wheeling and disappearing back into the thicket, snarling and growling. The report of the rifle echoed across the veld and then the thicket was still and silent.

A moment of recklessness and a poorly placed shot now left Cornie Coetzee facing perhaps the most dangerous scenario in all of African hunting: having to follow a wounded lion into dense cover. Cornie's client had shot the lion during the last moments of daylight, and it was far too dangerous to follow the wounded male into the thicket, especially without a team to back Cornie up in the event of a charge. As the fading light of day gave way to darkness, there was a grunt from within the thicket, then another. Finally, as the first stars appeared in the sky, the cat fell silent. Cornie and his client exited the blind and walked back to camp by the glow of the moon, holding their rifles close to them as they followed the sandy trail through the dim blue light. The tinny ring of the client's shot still echoed in their ears.

In the restless hours that followed, the hunters tried to sleep, unable to escape the reality that they would have to be on the wounded lion's spoor at first light. Cornie gathered his team—an assistant PH, a tracker, an

Lion populations in Namibia remain strong and stable, thanks in large part to the revenue generated by sport hunters. (Photo courtesy of Jofie Lamprecht)

agile fox terrier, and his client—and in the chill of predawn they headed for the water hole. With the tracker in the lead and Cornie following and covering him with his .416, the group started into the thicket where the lion had disappeared the evening before. Cornie and the rest were hoping they would find the lion dead in the mopane thicket, but after eighty yards of tracking, the group still had not found a trace of blood. The terrier worked its way along, following the invisible scent trail with growing enthusiasm. Cornie turned to his crew and told them to be ready for the possibility of a short-range charge in the thicket.

A grunt and a roar shocked the men to a standstill. There, for brief seconds, stood the lion between two thornbushes. The cat gave another guttural grunt, thrashed its tail left and right, and then slipped into the heavy cover at a trot.

When the lion vanished, the tracker, shaking at the sight of the cat at such close range, told Cornie that someone was going to get mauled and made it clear that he did not intend for it to be him despite the loss of pay. The tracker threw his hands up and made his way back out of the thicket toward the waiting hunting car. The rest of the group continued into the thicket, following the scant blood trail over the gray sand and watching the low thorn thickets for the flick of an ear or a twitching tail that might betray the lion's position. This time, the cat would almost surely come for them, and it would only be stopped with a well-placed bullet.

In the long moments that followed, Cornie, the assistant PH, and the client pressed deeper into the thicket with Cornie serving as tracker and lead gun in the likely event of a charge. The fox terrier, taking its cue from the tracker, had vanished from the thicket when the lion appeared and did not return. Slowly the men pressed deeper into the ever-tightening sea of thorns. Their soft-soled hunting shoes made no sound against the sandy earth as Cornie led them one step at a time deeper into the cover.

Another short series of grunts came from a wide thornbush directly ahead of the men. Cornie dropped to one knee, leveling his rifle and waiting for the inevitable. The lion roared again, still hidden in the

Cornie, his client, and a tremendous male lion. (Photo courtesy of Elaine Coetzee)

thick bush, and then exploded out of the thicket, tail churning, head cocked, and face twisted into a savage snarl as it rushed for the men. The twenty-five yards that separated the men and the lion shortened with each bound. Cornie leveled the .416, centered the sights on the lion's widening mouth, and pressed the trigger. The force of the bullet stopped the cat at once and sent it careering end-over-end in a somersault that left it dead at Cornie's feet. Cornie quickly shuffled backward and worked the bolt of his rifle to deliver an insurance shot.

Cornie covered the lion with the rifle until he was sure that it was dead and then turned to his crew, which had now dwindled to a single safari client, very pale, with a bewildered look on his face. The assistant PH, apparently taking his cue from the sage tracker and the wise terrier, had abandoned the thicket during the charge. Cornie stood alone with a trembling client who was too badly shaken even to run away.

Cornie found the tracker, the assistant PH, and the fox terrier back at the truck and told them that the lion was down and asked the men if they would be so kind as to return to their duties now that the lion

Nightfall over the plains of Namibia. (Photo courtesy of Jofie Lamprecht)

was officially out of commission. Soon the shock of the charge turned to elation for Cornie's client when he realized that they had secured a great old lion. Now that the business of the follow-up was finished, the men's drawn faces turned to smiles and the client received backslaps and handshakes.

But even among the celebrants there was an understanding that the whole hunt might have turned out very differently. Cornie's last-second shot had saved the day. The truth about hunting dangerous game is that one error can have permanent consequences. The best PHs make sure that their clients are protected, even if that means exposing themselves to great personal risk.

CHAPTER 9

A Reputation for Toughness

Professional hunter: Jaco van der Merwe
Location: Khomas Hochland

The herd of a dozen Hartmann zebras stopped just over a hundred yards from the hunters and stood close together. A thin column of dust rose behind them, stirred up by their churning hoofs during their gallop across the dry, rocky plains of the Khomas Hochland. Despite their striking black-and-white markings, zebras can sometimes be extremely difficult to see, especially when they stand at some distance or in the shade of heavy brush. This small band, however, was plainly visible among the broken thorn cover and rocky hills. The difficulty was in identifying which of the milling animals was the stallion.

Professional hunter Jaco van der Merwe soon saw the stallion clearly and urged his client, Frederic Brown, to grab the shooting sticks and aim for the animal's chest before the herd continued across the plains and out of sight. Frederic aligned the sights of his .404 Jeffery on the vertical line extending upward from the stallion's front leg and pressed the trigger when the sights settled. The big rifle roared and rose up nosefirst off the sticks with the recoil; the stallion also reacted to the shot, rising and turning in a half-circle as the 400-grain slug connected with its shoulder. The herd galloped across the plains, the stallion lagging behind the others. The trackers pointed and shouted in Afrikaans that they could see blood on the zebra's shoulder.

African game has a reputation for resisting punishment, even shots from heavy rifles. From the diminutive pygmy antelopes of the dark equatorial jungles to the members of the Big Five, African game has inherited a level of tenacity and toughness unmatched by animals on other continents. The most common explanation for this inherent toughness is continuous natural selection, a genetic weeding-out of the weak and unfit by Africa's harsh conditions and many large predators. This process of natural selection for toughness means African game

Hartmann mountain zebras live in the rocky hills of Namibia's central range. (Photo courtesy of Jacques Strauss)

can take a pounding that would flatten most animals. African game has grit, plain and simple.

Among Africa's toughest plains game are the continent's various varieties of zebras. Zebras are capable of withstanding a large amount of shock and damage while remaining on their feet and rapidly distancing themselves from pursuing hunters. A well-placed shot in the vitals will kill a zebra just as it will any other species, but shots outside the kill zone, even those that would cripple most other species, often result in a tedious follow-up or a lost trophy.

Namibia is home to a zebra subspecies found nowhere else on the continent. *Equus zebra hartmannae,* the Hartmann mountain zebra, is one of two extant mountain zebra species (the other is the Cape mountain zebra of South Africa), and it may be hunted only in Namibia's mountainous western regions. They live in gregarious herds made up of a dominant stallion leading a harem of up to two-dozen mares. Hunting for mountain zebras requires pursuing them in the rocky hill country and approaching within rifle range of the wary animals without being detected by the many ears, eyes, and noses in the herd. The mares are always on the alert for predators, scanning the horizon for movement while registering every scent on the passing breeze. There is little that is guaranteed when hunting for zebras, other than the fact that if you aren't good at stalking and an excellent shot, you won't get your trophy.

Despite the zebra's reputation for toughness, the .404 Jeffery Frederic used is plenty of gun for any plains-game animal. So Jaco and the others were shocked when the stallion absorbed the impact of the big bullet and galloped off across the dry plains and into the distant hills not far behind its harem of mares. Jaco could barely see the zebras as they were swallowed in the rising dust.

Frederic had recently undergone ankle surgery that precluded him from following the stallion into the rocky hills, so Jaco helped Frederic's wife, Mary, down from the truck. While Frederic stayed with the vehicle, Mary and Jaco would climb the mountain and would, in all likelihood, find the stallion dead on the rock-strewn ridge above them—that is, if Frederic's shot had hit where the trackers believed it had. Jaco handed the rifle to Mary and they set off into the rocky foothills in search of the stallion.

The blood spoor glistened in the midday sun. Tracking the stallion was easy, despite the overlapping half-moon tracks of the herd as the animals climbed the dusty slope, for the stallion had been in the back of the herd and had left red flashes of crimson scattered on the loose, gray rocks as it ascended the mountain just behind the mares. Jaco and his tracker worked the trail out, following the hoof marks of the stallion over the dry earth between boulders as large as the hunting car below them. Mary followed behind, holding Frederic's big rifle at the ready in case she needed to finish the zebra.

The trackers lowered themselves in the shade of a large rock and pointed at a rocky patch of open ground in the distance. The band of mares was standing in a loose circle among a field of boulders. The stallion, apparently hit hard, stood off by itself away from the others. Jaco ushered Mary to the front so that she could place the finishing shot on her husband's zebra. She shouldered the rifle, took aim over the express sights, and waited. So did Jaco.

He expected the shot at any moment, but something was wrong. Mary was examining the rifle, and it became clear to Jaco that since she had brought her own Thompson/Center Encore rifle on safari, she had no experience with the big .404 that her husband carried. In her frustration she handed the rifle to Jaco, who found the safety, lined up the sights on the stallion's shoulder, and fired. The recoil drove Jaco backward, but he plainly saw the stallion drop into the rocks below as if stricken by a lightning bolt from the blue sky above them. *That should do it,* he thought.

The herd thundered over the crest and into the canyon on the other side of the hill as Jaco gathered Mary and the tracker to go and fetch the zebra. They were smiling and talking about the hunt as they picked their way down the rocky slope toward the place where the zebra had gone down. The driver and Frederic heard the shot from the plains below and started to drive the truck around to meet them and help skin the stallion.

Jaco and the others continued down toward the nest of rocks where the zebra had fallen, but to their amazement they saw the stallion was on its feet again. Jaco cursed in astonishment as it started off down the mountain. Raising the rifle and swinging ahead of the running

At right: Hartmann zebras have striking markings that lack the shadow striping found on the more common zebra subspecies. (Photo courtesy of Benjamin Gettinger)

Jaco van der Merwe led his client, above, to this excellent stallion. Tough to find and bring down, Hartmann mountain zebras are one of Namibia's most exciting species to hunt. (Photo courtesy of Jaco van der Merwe/African Twilight Safaris)

zebra, Jaco touched off another round, firing with the precision of a seasoned marksman. The slug caught the stallion in the chest, but did not slow it. The zebra made its escape back down the face of the mountain and onto the rocky plains.

Jaco, Mary, and the tracker hurried down the mountain after the zebra, which was now running full-tilt across the plain toward the approaching hunting vehicle. Wondering how on earth an animal could take three 400-grain slugs to the chest and continue at such a clip, Jaco watched the zebra in disbelief. The stallion was running at full speed across the open plain, shrouded by a cloud of silvery dust raised by its churning hoofs. It kept a straight course across the plains toward the thorny hills beyond, never faltering or changing course. It ran within thirty yards of the hunting vehicle as the trackers waved and shouted in an effort to turn the zebra back. In a flash, it was past them, running at full stride over the dry Namibian plain.

Jaco, Mary, and the tracker reached the bottom of the hill and started in a trot toward the waiting vehicle. When they reached the car, Frederic was astounded to learn that the zebra he had seen run in front of them was the same stallion he had hit with the .404 earlier in the day. (He had no idea why the men in the truck were so feverishly pointing and shouting for him to fire despite the obvious handicap of being without his firearm.) Frederic was even more astounded to hear that the zebra had taken two more slugs to the chest and managed to bolt across the plains and disappear back into heavy cover with the herd.

Dusty, exhausted, and even more determined to put a stop to the chase, Jaco, Mary, Frederic, and the trackers set out through the dry

Jaco van der Merwe of African Twilight Safaris.

thorn forest after the stallion, which had slowed considerably. Shortly after they picked up the trail, they found the stallion, and Frederic was able to finish it with a fourth shot from his .404.

The ability to absorb the level of punishment the stallion withstood and continue on into heavy cover is a testament to the toughness of African animals. When the hunting party finally reached the zebra, they looked at the bullet holes in its shoulders. Frederic and Jaco had both hit the stallion in the chest and front shoulder, though both men missed breaking any bones.

They returned to camp worn out and covered in grime but with the joy of knowing the hunt had been difficult but successful. Frederic and Mary went on to take several other species on their safari with Jaco, but the memory of the marathon zebra hunt that led from the plains to the mountains of Khomas Hochland will remain a story to be relived and retold every time a new friend comments on their lovely zebra rug.

CHAPTER 10

The Homecoming Cat

Professional hunter: Tim Liedtke
Location: Erongo Mountains

Swakopmund, on Namibia's western coast, is an oasis during the country's hot months. Cold Atlantic breezes make the town a pleasant getaway from the hot, dry interior during the warmest months of the year, and the town is a favorite vacation destination for Namibians. Tim Liedtke, son of Gerd and Martina Liedtke, was enjoying his holiday in "Swakop," as it is often referred to, when a phone call cut his vacation plans short.

It was his brother, Ralf, who was back at the family's Okondura Ranch at the foot of the Erongo Mountains near Karibib. He told Tim that they had a problem developing near one of their cattle pens, for the spoor of a big leopard had been seen all around the perimeter of the kraal. Based on the evidence and the persistence with which the leopard had been trying to get into the cattle pen, it would only be a matter of time before the cat started killing calves.

Ralf's assessment was correct. Tim immediately left Swakop and headed back for Okondura, driving through the smooth silver dunes and over the peaks of the Erongos to arrive at the ranch the next day. By the time Tim arrived, the leopard had already struck.

Tim and Ralf stood looking at the spoor in a patch of sandy road near the cattle operation. It looked like a giant serpent had crossed the road. To the left and right of the smooth channel that the dead calf had left in the sand as the cat dragged it were spattered specks of blood. The tracks confirmed that this was, indeed, the same cat that had been prowling around the kraal the day before. Ralf and Tim believed that the cat was an old female, likely beyond reproductive age and perhaps unable to hunt wild prey.

The two men followed the trail from the sand road up into the tall winter-yellowed grass and scattered thorn. The waist-high foliage made it difficult to follow the path the cat took as it dragged the calf from the kraal into the thorns, where it had eaten its fill in the moonlight. A hundred yards into the heavy bush, the brothers came upon what remained of the calf. By morning, the cat had slipped back into the hills to spend the day, and all that remained of the calf was the head.

A cattle-killing leopard poses an obvious problem for a working ranch like Okondura. The Liedtke family had lived on the ranch for three generations, and they were among the first families to establish sport hunting on their extensive acreage. Today Okondura plays host to a number of international sport hunters each year, but a large percentage of the family's income still comes from their cattle operations. The economic impact of a marauding leopard could be severe. Tim and Ralf knew that they would have to deal with this cattle-killer.

The spoor of a large male leopard. (Photo courtesy of Gerard Erasmus)

There was not enough of the calf left to serve as bait, so Tim and Ralf returned to Okondura Lodge. Tired, thorn-torn, and powdered with dust, they sat together by the fire and talked about how they could find the leopard before it struck again. The cat had feasted and had left its kill to spend the daylight hours in the rocky hills, so it was unlikely that it would feed again that night. There was no way to track the leopard, and hound hunting had been outlawed in Namibia the year before. The brothers decided that the cat would likely come down from the hills and drink at a water hole a little more than a half-mile from the lodge.

As the first violet hint of sunlight cast faint shadows over the gray earth, Tim and Ralf arrived at the water hole. It was not long before they found prints pressed deep in the soft, white sand. They were very large for a female leopard, but they had the distinct oval shape that told the brothers this was indeed a female and not a young tom. The spoor led out of the grass and down to the water's edge. After drinking its fill by the light of the moon, the cat had turned back, its tracks disappearing at the edge of the tall grass.

The leopardess vanished for the next few days, patrolling the low, rocky hills and leaving only as a set of large, oval prints at the edge of the water hole. Tim decided the best bet would be to place a bait for the cat near the water. He hoped the leopard would find it and stay long enough for Tim or Ralf to get a shot. The brothers selected a stout tree in a relatively open patch of ground near the water hole and secured the carcass of a warthog in a low-hanging branch. With their bait set and the sun fading quickly, there was nothing for the brothers to do but wait for the cat to return.

That evening, as Ralf returned to the truck, Tim loaded his .30-06 and climbed into a tree a hundred yards away from the warthog. The bait tree was plainly visible through the scattered thorns and acacias that surrounded the water hole. If the leopard came to it during daylight hours, Tim would have a clean shot while the cat was silhouetted against the branch. Now there was nothing left to do but wait.

Hours passed as Tim sat in the tree, resting his arms on the rifle in front of him. The sun sank toward the mountains, and long shadows stretched out from the trees and grass. The plains were quiet and still in the long afternoon hours, but as nightfall approached, game began to appear. In the distance, a group of springboks filtered out of the thorns well beyond the bait tree, moving cautiously through the tall grass on slender legs toward the water hole. The herd moved in broken order out of the bush, their heads rising and falling as they tested the dry air for any scent of danger. Tim watched the springbok herd and then turned his focus back to the water's edge, alert for any other animals to approach.

When Tim looked back at the herd, he saw that the springboks had stopped and were standing with their attention focused on the long grass just ahead and to their right. One member whistled an alarm and all of the springboks turned, scattering back into the thorn cover while shouting their high, shrill alarm calls over the plains.

Tim readied himself, pulling his Blaser 93 rifle into position and resting the black stock on a limb ahead of him. He was certain that the springboks must have seen or winded the leopard, and Tim tried to calm himself as he watched the bait tree through his Swarovski scope. Daylight was quickly fading and the shadow of the sun setting behind the hills crept out over the plains like an inky flood, making it difficult to see the warthog in the tree.

In the fading light, Tim saw a dark form slipping out of the bush, twenty yards from the bait. From its size and movements, Tim believed that it was a duiker, but after he raised his field glasses Tim was shocked to find that the dark form was, in fact, a leopard slipping down toward the water. Making as little noise as possible, Tim rested the rifle in a steady position and lowered his face until his cheek was gently touching the cold, black stock of the Blaser. The cat appeared in the scope, growing larger with each step. Tim had to wait as the cat was quartering toward him and moving, and there was no good shot. The cat disappeared behind a short, squatty thornbush and there was

The thick bush and thornveld of Namibia is home to large numbers of leopards. Educated from generations of preying on domestic cattle, these cats are difficult to find. (Photo courtesy of Jacques Strauss)

no movement for some time. Then the cat broke cover again, slipping along the water's edge and out of sight.

Just as Tim realized he was not going to get a shot at the cat at all, a second dark form appeared almost where the first had been. It was another leopard, a female that was even larger than the first. Through the Swarovski scope Tim examined this second leopard. It appeared old, and he could plainly tell after watching it through the scope that it was neither pregnant nor nursing. This was the cat they were after.

Tim settled in behind the rifle and found the cat's spotted shoulder through the cross hairs. In the dim light he picked a single black rosette on the cat's shoulder, centered the rifle, and pressed the trigger. The Blaser jumped with the recoil of the shot and a flash of fire from the muzzle blinded Tim, preventing him from seeing anything in the growing darkness. As the shot echoed, he heard

Tim Liedtke and the homecoming cat. (Photo courtesy of Gerd Liedtke/Okondura Ranch)

the roaring and snarling of a cat in the darkness, but he could not be certain which cat it was.

Ralf had heard the shot and immediately came in the hunting truck. Tim was relieved to see the bobbing yellow lamps of the headlights cutting through the thorns. It was fully dark by then, and the first stars were shimmering in the sky overhead as Tim slipped down from the tree and told his brother what had happened. They climbed into the truck and started toward the sandy ground on the opposite side of the water hole, driving slowly. The Liedtke brothers had both grown up in the bush and were far too smart to trail a wounded leopard into the thorns and rocks in the darkness. If the cat had gone, they would have to wait until morning to follow it.

There was no waiting necessary, though. As the headlights cut through the grass, Tim saw a flattened patch of grass. There, lying almost where it had been when the rifle fired, was the dead leopard.

Just as the brothers had thought, it was a very old cat without any cubs. Its tracks matched those they had seen at the kraal and beside the dead calf. The brothers had succeeded in stopping the marauding cat before it killed more stock. That night when they returned to the lodge there was cause for celebration, for Tim and Ralf had managed to outwit Africa's deadliest and most cunning predator.

CHAPTER II

The Last Shot

Professional hunter: Jacques Strauss
Location: Kalahari

In the last light of evening, Jacques Strauss lay in the shade of a blackthorn tree and watched as a herd of kudu bulls crossed the open ground in front of him. One kudu, an old bull with deep curls and long ivory tips, stopped less than fifty yards away from where Jacques lay with his rifle close beside him. Moving silently over the green plains, the old bull approached a stand of green thorns and began slowly browsing. The other bulls moved silently through the brush just ahead of Jacques. The evening sun shone brilliantly off the smooth brown curls of the bulls' horns as the herd, unaware of his presence, made its way past the waiting hunter.

Jacques wasn't after a kudu, though. Despite their majesty and the thrill of their sudden appearance in the evening light, Jacques was content to watch the majestic gray bulls pass by him. The string of kudu bulls that continued to edge closer to Jacques actually presented him with a major problem: The oryx herd he was after was feeding directly behind the kudu.

Jacques had spotted the oryxes a mile back: four dun-colored bodies with contrasting black-and-white facial features and long black horns moving across the green plains on his family's Kowas Farm at the edge of the Kalahari. One of the oryxes, an old cow, had badly bent horns. Upon seeing the cow, Jacques decided to remove it from the gene pool and prevent future generations of oryxes from suffering the same odd affliction. In doing so, he would also provide meat for the entire Strauss family and the team of trackers, skinners, cooks, and laundry staff that worked at Kowas.

His otherwise brilliant stalk on the oryx had been temporarily foiled by the wandering band of kudu bulls. If Jacques didn't manage to slip around the kudus, it would be dark and he would never get his chance at the oryx. Having already pushed his luck as far as he could,

The oryx is adapted to surviving on very little water. Also known as gemsbok, the oryx in Namibia sport horns that sometimes exceed forty inches in length. (Photo courtesy of Jacques Strauss)

Jacques would have to wait for an opportunity to develop. He hoped it would not be long.

The old oryx cow slipped out of the brush in a clearing not far beyond the scattered kudu herd. Jacques knew that this would be the only chance he would get at the old cow before the sun set. Rising slowly, he rested his 7x64 rifle on the shooting sticks and centered the cross hairs of his scope on the old cow's shoulder. Knowing that the kudu bulls had probably seen him and would soon sound the alarm, Jacques steadied his rifle, held his breath, and fired.

After the report of the rifle, Jacques clearly heard the heavy thump of the 180-grain softpoint hitting the oryx. The old cow wheeled and started into heavy cover, disappearing in the fading light.

Jacques was not sure of his shot, and he wanted to begin tracking the oryx immediately. When he found blood, Jacques squatted and rubbed it between his fingers. It was thin and watery—possibly a gut shot, and not a good sign at this late hour. He continued, moving cautiously and covering the trail ahead with his rifle in case the oryx ran. Jacques tried not to think about the very real likelihood that he could come up on the wounded oryx in heavy cover. If he did, there was the possibility it would charge. Having grown up in a hunting family, Jacques knew that catching the horns of a wounded oryx could be just as deadly as stepping on an adder or facing a charging lion.

The trail opened into a wide, green plain where two oryxes stood between clumps of thorn looking over their backtrail. When Jacques saw them, he raised his field glasses but did not see any sign of blood on either oryx as they turned and galloped full speed into the thorns and were lost in the dim light. That was all that he could do for the night. Without a support team or a light, Jacques could go no farther until dawn. He turned and headed back toward his truck, heartsick over the possibility of losing the oryx.

As the sun set and a chorus of jackals welcomed the coming of the night, Jacques tried to imagine what could have happened. Had the bullet failed? He had seen a bush just in front of the oryx. Was it possible that he could have clipped a limb with his bullet? He would spend long, sleepless hours that night replaying every possible scenario.

Dawn broke warm and green over the plains. The wet-season rains had been abundant, and all across the savanna, which is dry and brittle for much of the hunting season, the grass and trees were emerald green with rainy-season growth. Beautiful as it was, the new greenery would make tracking the wounded oryx all the more difficult.

Jacques enlisted the aid of Kowas's seasoned tracker, Petrus, to help him find the wounded oryx. Together they went back to the place where

Jacques Strauss resting in the shade while on safari in the Kalahari. (Photo courtesy of Jacques Strauss)

Jacques had left the shooting sticks the night before—the last place where he had seen blood. The dried blood on the broken grass was wet again with the dew, and as the sun rose the pair began following the scattered blood drops through the plains, walking past great stands of camelthorn acacia and wicked blackthorn bushes.

Petrus moved ahead in the tall grass, slipping silently left and right on the scattered trail as Jacques followed behind and watched the cover ahead of them for any sign of the cow. Both of them tried not to remember all of the stories they had heard of African hunters stumbling on a wounded oryx and the awful goring many had received when the long black stiletto horns impaled their bodies. It was best to be cautious when following an oryx, for a wounded oryx was unpredictable, fearless, and well equipped to wreak havoc with its deadly horns and hoofs. Even the best hunters could suddenly find themselves badly injured and far away from help.

The Kalahari in spring. (Photo courtesy of Jacques Strauss)

Jacques and Petrus with the old oryx that Strauss killed seconds before it charged. (Photo courtesy of Jacques Strauss)

The trail narrowed as walls of thorns began to hem the men in. Petrus pointed to the zigzagging blood trail that indicated the oryx was looking for a place to lie down. In all likelihood the cow would be close-by, hidden in the thick thorns and ready to charge. Jacques would have to be ready to shoot quickly, and he would have to make the first shot count. He pulled the bolt of his rifle back, looking down to watch as the bolt lifted a cartridge from the magazine and fed it into the chamber. The bolt shut with a firm click and, with his finger resting against the safety catch, Jacques moved to his left to be sure that if the oryx ran he could get a shot without worrying about Petrus's position in the thorns.

There was a shudder in the low green thorns that brought the rifle to Jacques's shoulder with a snap. A slender jackal trotted out ten yards ahead of him and then veered off onto the plains, galloping a short distance over the green grass and then stopping under a low-growing thornbush. The jackal did not go any farther; it stood watching Jacques, its small round eyes unblinking as it studied the man with the rifle. Jacques knew that he had found the jackal because the two of them were following the same blood trail. Now the jackal stood at attention, its foxy face frozen in an anticipatory look of interest in what was about to happen. To Jacques, the jackal's presence was a clear indicator that the oryx was very close.

Jacques slipped the safety off and started to step forward into the bush when he heard a rustling and saw the dun-colored body of the oryx as it stood and focused its gaze on Petrus. Unarmed and well within range of the cow, there was nothing that Petrus could do as the wounded oryx lowered its head and prepared to charge.

Jacques steadied the cross hairs on the oryx's black-and-white head and pressed the trigger. The 180-grain bullet hit exactly where it was aimed, and the cow dropped dead before it could charge the helpless tracker.

"That was the right move, Jacques," Petrus said, still shaken at the thought of what might have been. When their nerves calmed, the men stood over the oryx and looked at its bent horns and the two bullet holes. One, Jacques' first, had been a bit far back. The second, however, had been right on target.

CHAPTER 12

THE BUFF OF THE BERG

Professional hunter: Jofie Lamprecht
Location: Waterberg Plateau

By the time the sun was up, Jofie Lamprecht of Hunters Namibia Safaris and his client, Alexander, were already on the crest of the Waterberg Plateau, a huge massif that rises abruptly from the otherwise flat landscape of Namibia's central plain. Their ascent up the Waterberg from the lower elevations brought them up over red rock walls formed by sand piles that had petrified over millennia to form a great, elevated table high above the surrounding grasslands. The Waterberg had once been a sacred place to the Herero people, and it was there that many of them were killed by Germans in the Herero massacre of the early twentieth century. As the sun rose over the eastern desert, it made the rock pilings and loose sand of the Waterberg appear blood-red.

It was April, and the heat and rains of fall were giving way to cooler, drier conditions. The hunting party, led by Jofie's tracker and hunting assistant, Abiud, set out on foot just after sunrise. Jofie hoped to put his client onto a massive Waterberg buffalo bull as soon as possible. They had covered several miles of thorny veld under the rising heat of midmorning before Abiud halted them with an outstretched hand and lowered himself over a series of heart-shaped buffalo tracks. The buffaloes had crossed from a watering hole into thick cover early in the morning.

Finding the tracks so quickly was great luck, but following buffaloes into heavy cover always carried with it an element of danger. As they worked their way into the heavy Terminalia bush, Abiud caught sight of one of the buffaloes and tried to quiet the hunters, but it was too late. The buffalo herd, fanned out within the thick, green tangles, had executed a maneuver Lamprecht nicknamed the "Crazy Ivan"—the entire herd turned in a 270-degree arc after entering the bush so they would spot anything that was following them. They were lying in the Terminalia in much the same way a large bass waits under a fallen log

Professional hunter and photographer Jofie Lamprecht closes in on a buffalo bull. (Photo courtesy of Jofie Lamprecht)

to ambush prey. When the hunters approached, the herd rose from the thick cover and trotted out across the open plain, the sound of their thundering hoofs blending with the cracking and snapping of thorns as the entire group plowed through the thicket toward more open country. Jofie watched the running buffaloes as they disappeared behind a red veil of dust.

Shortly before Namibia's independence from South Africa, the Waterberg Plateau, which covers almost ninety thousand acres, was named a nature preserve. The plateau is an ideal habitat for large ruminants. Not only is the top of the plateau isolated from the rest of the central plains, but it is also a unique microclimate that remains much greener and wetter than the surrounding plains for much of the year. Herds of elands were transplanted to the park so that they would be protected from poachers by the sheer walls of the massif. Soon roans and sables were introduced to the park. Black and white rhinos were released as well.

Cape buffaloes, too, were brought into the park, and today they thrive atop the massif despite the fact that buffaloes are normally not allowed south of the "red line," a boundary that prevents buffaloes from entering areas where cattle are ranched in an effort to quell the spread of infections like hoof-and-mouth disease. The red line lies hundreds of miles north of the Waterberg, but the unique geography of the Waterberg makes it possible for wild herds of buffaloes to survive there without posing a threat to cattle.

Hunting on the Waterberg Plateau was very limited until 2003 when the last private lease of the park ended and hunting ceased on the plateau altogether. It was not until 2009 that the government of Namibia once again offered the Waterberg for lease, and hunting rights for the region were auctioned to Hunters Namibia Safaris.

As the dust from the departing herd settled, Jofie, Alexander, and Abiud set out on the spoor. The herd had crossed the open, sandy plain and had vanished once again into a forest of thick Terminalia, making for slow tracking. Abiud led the way into the shadowy cover with Jofie close behind. The rainy season had recently ended and there were no dry leaves to crackle underfoot as there would be later in the season. But the rains had brought with them new growth, and the green thickets were difficult to navigate and impossible to move through silently.

The hunters spent long hours dogging the herd, chasing buffaloes that knew they were being pursued. The buffaloes moved for miles over the fenceless open plains and thick, thorny tangles of the Waterberg, always remaining just out of reach of the men. By the time the sun began to set, Jofie and the others were exhausted and powdered in a fine coating of red dust accumulated during the miles of tracking under the April sun. Jofie gave the order to stop. They would head back to camp and start fresh in the morning.

Over the course of the following week, the hunting party spent long days stalking buffaloes on the plateau without any luck. Despite having found tracks almost immediately after arriving, the men had no luck connecting with a big bull. They covered many dusty miles, churning the red sand with their boots as they slipped though the overhanging boughs of Terminalia in search of the herds.

The Waterberg's other game animals were plentiful, including the princely sables with their jet-black coats and long, ridged horns

The final moments with Jofie closing in on a big Cape buffalo in heavy cover. (Photo courtesy of Jofie Lamprecht)

that glimmered under the midday sun. Trophy elands and roans were also seen frequently during the hunt, but the great herds of buffaloes kept largely out of sight in the heaviest cover, limiting their movements to nighttime travels in search of fresh grazing and water. In April it was still wet enough atop the plateau that the herds could drink at several watering points regularly.

To have any chance of connecting with one of the Waterberg bulls, Jofie and the others had to continue their daily patrols over the miles of red sand. Each day, the party cut the tracks of buffalo herds, sometimes following two groups in a single day, but the unpredictable winds and the heavy cover on the rim of the Waterberg ensured that the buffaloes always managed to hear or smell the hunters before they could approach for a shot.

By April, most of the rain has moved out of central Namibia. Infrequent storms do occur in the region, however, and as Jofie and Abiud watched the gathering western clouds turn from pale white to gunmetal gray, they knew they would be caught in one of these rare

The Waterberg Plateau is one of the few places in Namibia where Cape buffalo can be hunted. (Photo courtesy of Jacques Strauss)

late-season squalls. Soon the first raindrops fell over the plateau, and then the storm broke and the water came as a white wall, sweeping the Waterberg as the hunters huddled, frustrated, under the same weeping wattle trees that the buffaloes favored for escaping the heat of the midday sun.

When the rain passed and the sun returned, the soaked hunters set out again, hoping that the rain would change their luck. With the water still dripping from the twisted branches of the trees and the last grim clouds hanging on the eastern horizon, the men set out in single file once again and started across the rim of the plateau. Soon Abiud stopped the group with an upturned hand. Two hulking black buffaloes turned and charged into the bush, shaking the water from the branches as they passed into deeper cover.

The men slowed their stalk and followed Abiud, who stooped over the fresh tracks while Jofie and Alexander watched the trail ahead for any piece of a buffalo—a curve of horn, a ragged ear, or the hulking mass of a bull's shoulder hiding among the interlocking green arms of the Terminalia. By the time the last of the storm clouds passed and the sun returned, the men were deep in the thick, green cover and the only sounds were the dripping of water from the low-hanging branches and the wet, sloppy squishing of the men's feet inside their leather boots.

Abiud stopped them once more with a wave of his thin hand. There, just ahead in the trail, was the head of a buffalo and one sweeping black hook of a horn. Jofie leaned toward his client, but it was too late. The buffalo tossed its head, snorted, and charged off into the green thorn thicket yet again.

With each failed stalk, the men were one day closer to ending the safari without a buffalo in the salt. But Jofie knew that there were exceptional buffaloes within the boundaries of the park, and if their luck changed, Alexander would have his chance at an outstanding bull.

As it turned out, that chance came on the last day, just hours before the end of the hunt. Jofie and Alexander were walking along the rim

Jofie and his client, Alexander, and the outstanding bull they took on the Waterberg Plateau. (Photo courtesy of Jofie Lamprecht)

of the plateau, looking down at the plain below. Abiud stopped and leaned over a set of fresh prints in the red sand. Two buffalo bulls had passed by not long before. For Jofie and Alexander, the fresh spoor represented their last chance to take a bull on the Waterberg. The tracks were large, but Jofie wouldn't have any idea how big the bulls were until he caught up to them, and with the sun setting low over the western horizon, every moment was critical.

The group set out through the Terminalia in single file, slipping silently through the dense cover. Abiud turned to Jofie and told him that the big bull and his askari, or younger companion bull, were headed for a water hole at the far edge of the thicket. The hunters quickened their pace and headed directly for the water in an effort to catch the bulls before they vanished into heavier cover.

As the shadows stretched over the tall rock spires at the edge of the plateau forming a network of darkness and purple light, the men stooped at the edge of an open patch of ground within a large tract of green cover. Abiud was once more in front, squatting as he watched the young askari bull moving through the opening just ahead. Although its horns already sported a fine curl, its bosses had not yet grown together, and the helmetlike area between the horns was still soft. From the grass beside the askari, the larger bull emerged, its thick black horns dropping in deep curls that were wider than its shoulders. The horns rose up beside the bull's face, and where the bosses met, the horn was the color and texture of dried volcanic rock. This was an extraordinary bull.

Jofie pulled his client close beside him in the fading light and told him to place a bullet right in the middle of the bull's shoulder as quickly as he could. Alexander's .375 erupted with a flash of red as the 350-grain Woodleigh bullet found its mark, the heavy thump of bullet against flesh clearly audible amid the echoing crack of the rifle. The bull turned, tail high, and started off in a slow canter with the askari following closely behind.

The old bull that Alexander had shot was already slowing when it reached denser cover, and Jofie and the others found it piled up less than fifty yards from where it had been shot. The group stayed back, paying careful attention to the bull's younger companion, which appeared as a dark shadow circling the perimeter of the thorn forest. Eventually the askari grunted and ran off alone, crashing through the dark thorns until it was out of hearing. Alexander, Jofie, and Abiud stood examining the huge old bull where it had fallen nosefirst into the red sand.

After admiring the trophy and skinning the bull, they cleaned the skull. Then came the moment they were all waiting for. As they stretched the tape over the 45-inch horns, Jofie's hopes were confirmed. The bull of the Berg was the new record Namibian buffalo, and it ranked in the top fifty buffaloes of all time.

Around the time that Alexander shot his bull, one of Jofie's trail cameras captured an image of another massive Waterberg buffalo that would outscore even Alexander's monster bull. The story of the hunt for that bull remains, as yet, unwritten.

CHAPTER 13

THE CATTLE KILLER

Professional hunter: Hannes du Plessis
Location: Central Plateau

By the light of the narrow moon, the leopard slipped along the edge of the steel wires on the south side of the kraal, a pen built to house livestock. The cat could smell the cattle within the confines of the kraal, and it approached with its body low against the dusty ground. Despite its ferocious temperament and uncanny speed and strength, the leopard could not pull down one of the 1,200-pound heifers that stood lowing in the moonlight just beyond the heavy-gauge wires. Seeking an easier target, the tom worked back around the pen, its belly almost touching the sand as it slipped silently through the wires and waited.

Since the cat was downwind, the cattle that stood blinking slowly in the dim blue light had no idea that the tom was pressed flat against the cool sand within two bounds of their perimeter. The leopard moved without sound, slipping closer and closer to the cattle until it spotted what it was seeking in the moonlight. It was a calf, not much bigger than the tom. The leopard stopped, gathering its legs under it in the darkness, ready to attack. In two bounds, the cat was on the calf, spinning its body in the darkness as it caught hold of the calf's throat. The rest of the cattle rose and rushed around the confines of the kraal in a blind and futile panic.

It was the ninth of November when Hannes du Plessis received the call about the cattle-killing leopard. The farmer told Hannes what had happened the night before: A big tom leopard had slipped out of the Terminalia thicket that extended to the edge of the kraal and had made its way through the wires. When the cat had its victim secured, it dragged the calf back through the steel wires and into the thicket. Once hidden, the leopard had chosen a suitable tree and hoisted the calf up into the lowest branches. The cat had fed through the night on the rear loins of the calf and then slipped away from the tree at sunup. It was just after dawn

Leopard waits in the tall grass. (Photo courtesy of Jofie Lamprecht)

when the landowner found the remains of the calf a dozen feet up a thorny acacia. As the heat of day warmed the plains, glossy-green bottle flies found the calf and landed one by one on the exposed flesh. By that time, the leopard was long gone.

Hannes had the option to bring in a client to hunt for the leopard if he chose to since the cat was a known stock killer. Hannes offered the hunt to his client, Vincent Rehm, who was hunting for plains game. Fully aware of the rare opportunity he had been presented, Vincent agreed to postpone his plains-game hunt to go in search of a more deadly prize.

The staff at Hannes's Bergzicht lodge moved at a frenetic pace to load the vehicles with supplies for the leopard hunt. Hannes ordered Vincent to pack for two days, and led him out to re-zero his rifle from two hundred yards to seventy. It was unlikely that the cat would present a shot much farther away than one hundred yards. If things went terribly wrong, it might even have to be shot at much closer range.

They found the calf in the crotch of the tree where the cat had left it. Hannes backed away to avoid contaminating the area with human scent, a dead giveaway to the cat that its kill had been discovered. Hannes's men began constructing a blind from the dry branches and tall grass scattered in the thorn forest. The men built the blind about seventy yards away from the tree, hoping that the wind would not change and that the leopard would return to the kill. Chances were good that it would, as the cat had only eaten lightly. The only trick would be to get the cat there while the hunters were in the blind and while there was still enough light to shoot.

Hannes and his men built the blind without making any unnecessary noise, communicating mostly by waving hands and pointing fingers. The more disturbed the area was, Hannes knew, the less likely it would be that the cat would return. Hannes and his men worked quickly, constructing the blind in short order from the abundant winter grass and acacia that grew around the bait tree. Soon the blind was finished, and Hannes sent his men off with the radio. If the leopard happened to be watching or listening from some distance away (which was not at all unlikely), Hannes wanted to give the cat the impression that the men who came in search of his kill were leaving. The cat would not notice that two of the men had stayed behind at the kill site unless it heard, saw, or smelled them. There was nothing for Hannes and Vincent to do but wait.

The inside of a leopard blind is like no place else on earth. The initial moments are filled with the anxiety of knowing that the cat may be near and may appear at any moment. Hannes coached his client about what to expect. They both knew how graphic the results of a bad shot on a leopard could be.

“Don’t rush,” Hannes told him. “Wait for your shot and be sure it hits its mark.”

The men settled down, checking every branch and dry plant stem to be sure there would be no sound when Vincent moved into position for the shot. Hours passed in the cool dryness of the late-winter afternoon. The anxiety of being inside a leopard blind gave way to the exhaustion of waiting and hoping that the cat would come. It didn’t. Time passed, and the sun sank low without any sign that the cat would return to feed on the calf before sunset. The shadows softened and lengthened. The light gave the landscape a golden aura as the sun sank lower into the fold of the horizon.

At dusk, Hannes stiffened, leaning to look out at the limb where the calf rested. Three jackals had appeared at the base of the bait tree. In silent frustration, the jackals walked around the tree, tilting their heads occasionally to catch the scent of the meat or to ponder some method to retrieve it. The men watched the jackals circling the base of the tree and eyeing the calf that hung above. Suddenly, however, the jackal cohort grew wary as they watched the thornbush around them. All three jackals fixed their attention on the thicket just behind the bait tree. Something stirred, and the jackals galloped off silently down the game trail that had led them to the tree.

Hannes leaned forward toward the porthole in the wall of the blind for a better look. Vincent leaned, too, and saw, silhouetted against the sky, the form of a large tom leopard standing over its kill in the fork of the tree. Neither of the men had heard so much as the rasping of claws on bark. The leopard was suddenly there, straddling its kill and watching the surrounding thorns, silhouetted against the purple sky that exists only in the brief moments between the passing of day and the coming of night.

Vincent calmed himself with two deep breaths. Still, he was not certain that he could place his bullet correctly since the cat had moved into the tree without feeding. Vincent waited, feeling the heavy pressure of a rare opportunity about to vanish. And soon the leopard did vanish, disappearing back into the thorn without a sound, as suddenly and silently as it had arrived.

The landscape fell silent after the leopard disappeared from the tree. Could it have smelled us? Hannes wondered. No, the wind was right. The blind was positioned so that it was almost invisible and built out of natural materials. Had they made a sound? No, there had been no sound to alert the tom. The leopard, it seemed, had simply felt uncomfortable—perhaps it had sensed it was being watched—and vanished. Whatever the reason, the cat was gone. The best option at that point was to wait for the cat in the blind all night and hope to catch it feeding at dawn. It would be too difficult to try to return in the morning. Hunter and client settled back and tried to find a position that was reasonably comfortable (or at least less agonizing) to wait out the darkness.

The moon rose and crested, illuminating the long hours of darkness. The warmth of day faded, and the night turned and cold and still. From the blind, the men could hear the sounds of the night animals—jackals, honey badgers, and skunks—as they came by the blind and shuffled off into the black cloak of thorn that surrounded the bait. Sleep came in spurts for the men as they sat half-upright in the narrow blind. They tried to stay awake, tried to maintain focus so that they would be aware if the cat returned. But the long hours until dawn weighed heavily on the men, their focus faded, and they slipped in and out of sleep. The cold, hard earth numbed their legs and backs as they tried to get comfortable, exhausted after the long day.

It was not yet dawn when Hannes heard the scrape of claws against wood and was suddenly fully awake, his senses alerted by the sound of the cat climbing into the tree. By the dim light of the half-moon, the cat had made its way silently along the narrow game trails that wound through the thorns and was now just in front of them in the darkness. Hannes listened to the sounds of the cat pulling itself up onto the bait and then was chilled by a sudden silence. He could almost see the leopard in the blackness ahead of them. Hannes knew that the cat was standing over the bait, studying the starlit savanna with cold eyes. But there was no sound. Not a whisper, not the slightest pull on the meat nor the muffled sound of paws and claws adjusting on the limb. Nothing. Hunter and prey sat seventy yards apart, separated only by the darkness, and waited.

Finally Hannes heard the cat start feeding on the bait. When he knew the cattle killer had committed itself fully to eating, Hannes nudged Vincent. It was still before dawn and the eastern horizon had only begun to lighten. It would be some time before shooting light, and the men were forced to sit together in the narrow blind, shivering against the cold and listening to the tearing flesh as the cat fed. Periodically the cat would stop, perhaps taking time to study the surrounding area or to readjust its position.

For long moments the men sat watching the horizon as the sun began to cast a dull, gunmetal-gray haze over the desert landscape. They heard the far-off yap of a jackal and the songs of morning birds that were beginning to call, oblivious to the deadly waiting game occurring in the grove of acacias. Finally Hannes looked back at the tree and saw the silhouette of the leopard, its large head and muscular shoulders tearing at the bait. He gave Vincent the go-ahead.

To the naked eye, the leopard was nothing more than a black silhouette moving along the branch that held the bait. But as Vincent rested his cheek on the cold stock of his rifle and looked through his scope, he could see the details of the leopard clearly—the heavy body, the muscular forearms that ripped meat, and the round, predatory eyes that scanned the coming daylight as the leopard paused in its feeding. When the cross hairs of the scope came to rest on the cat's shoulder, Vincent took a breath, pressed his finger against the crescent of the trigger, and fired.

Leopard with impala kill. (Photo courtesy of Dirk de Bod)

In the dim light of dawn, the flash of the rifle burst forth as a red spray of flame from the muzzle. It blinded both Vincent and Hannes, the image of the muzzle flash etched into their blinking eyes as they heard a growl and the dull thump of the cat hitting the ground.

"I hope that got him," Vincent said.

"Me, too," Hannes replied with an earnest nod. No sensible PH wanted to follow a wounded leopard into the long grass, especially in dim light.

Vincent wanted to go with Hannes to find the cat, but Hannes refused. It was impossible to say where the leopard was and how badly the cat was wounded, and Hannes, as PH, was charged with the duty of finding the cat without putting his client at risk. Hannes stepped out of the blind and started toward the tree, pausing when he saw the spotted body lying at the base of the tree. He shot once, then a second time, to elicit a response. There was none. Hannes then called back to his client, and Vincent exited the blind. Together they approached the dead tom, which lay stretched at full length under the tree. Vincent's shot had done the trick.

In the warm light of morning, they celebrated the hunt and the great cat that Vincent had taken, which weighed almost 155 pounds. It was a fantastic addition to the trophies Vincent took while on his safari with Hannes. The farmer who lost the calf received recompense from the leopard hunt, helping to offset the financial loss from the calf. The system discourages farmers from indiscriminately shooting, trapping, or poisoning any leopard in the vicinity; hunting places value on predators that would otherwise be eradicated in farming communities. Instead, Vincent and Hannes had the opportunity to share a unique experience in their quest for the cattle-killer.

CHAPTER 14

The Beast

Hunting professional: Marina Lamprecht
Location: Kalahari

All Marina Lamprecht wanted was a look at the herd of red hartebeests she had been pursuing for several hours. The problem was that her professional hunter, who was also her son Jofie, had stopped on the trail just ahead of her and she could not see anything around his broad shoulders. When she started to step out of line with him, Jofie turned and looked back toward her to indicate that she should stay behind him to avoid spooking the hartebeests.

The sun was high and the Kalahari had been a long time without rain. Jofie's leather Russell hunting boots stirred small dust devils that spiraled up and faded in the afternoon heat just in front of Marina's face. Slowly the pair made their way forward, keeping the hartebeest herd in sight as they moved through the scattered trunks of the crooked camelthorn trees. The bull was ahead of them, standing with the herd of cows and calves in the yellow Kalahari grass just out of rifle range.

For many hunters traveling to Africa, part of the lure of the Dark Continent is adventure in an unknown, foreign land. But for Marina Lamprecht, hunting with her son on their Rooikraal Ranch in the Kalahari was anything but exotic. In fact, Rooikraal was the same place she had raised Jofie and her other children. Hunting was new to Marina. The business of hunting, however, was not.

"There are professional hunters, and then there are hunting professionals," Marina said. "Both play an equally important role in protecting the right to hunt locally, as well as promoting Africa as a hunting destination internationally. My husband and son are the former, and I am the latter."

Since establishing Hunters Namibia Safaris on Rooikraal in 1980 (when Jofie was just a year old), Marina had been involved in virtually every aspect of safari hunting. She helped her husband, Joof, set up camps; she cooked meals; and she trained staff to carry out the many tasks involved in operating a hunting camp. She also served on several committees and was involved with professional hunting organizations such as NAPHA, the Namibian Professional Hunters Association. Over the past thirty years, she had marketed her hunting company and Namibian hunting around the world, frequently attending trade shows in the United States and Europe to bolster interest in the safari industry.

The one aspect of the hunting industry that Marina was not familiar with, however, was hunting. While performing the duties of administrator for Hunters Namibia and helping oversee The Gun Shop, her husband's Windhoek-based firearms store and one of the largest firearms retail businesses in Namibia, Marina had very little time to actually go afield herself.

Joof had put together a special rifle for her in 1985. It was a Mannlicher Schoenauer bolt-action rifle in 6.5x54 with a full-length walnut stock, dual set triggers, and a buttplate door that opened to reveal a cleaning rod and oil canister concealed within the stock. Marina's rifle was topped with a Swarovski 4X32 scope locked to the receiver with an EAW claw mount. It was a superb hunting rig and a truly classic rifle, perfect for midsize game on the plains of the Kalahari. The problem was that Marina had never had time to take her rifle afield.

That changed one afternoon when Chris, Joof and Marina's son-in-law, returned from a hunt with Joof and recounted the story of his successful day afield. Marina took note of the fervor in Chris's voice as he sat in the lodge at Rooikraal and shared the details of the hunt over the braai. As the firelight rose and fell against the gray stone walls of the lodge, Marina began to imagine herself out on the hunt, scanning the open spaces of the vast, untouched Kalahari and stalking game the way that her husband and son did. Marina's mind was made up. She would give hunting a try.

Joof decided that it would be wise if his wife learned to hunt from someone other than her husband, and Jofie agreed that it would be best for familial relations if he was the one that took his mother on her first hunting trip. So it was settled. Marina would try her hand

Red hartebeests at a water hole. (Photo courtesy of Jacques Strauss)

at safari hunting, guided by her own son in the open grasslands and acacia forests of Rooikraal.

The vast, rolling, red-sand hills of the Kalahari made an impressive backdrop for Marina's initial foray into hunting. Rooikraal is situated among thousands of acres of prime Kalahari habitat. Camelthorn acacia trees, which stay green late into the spring, stand out in stark contrast to the rolling miles of yellow grass and open patches of rust-colored sand. It appears no living thing could survive out on the waterless savanna, but in fact the Kalahari is home to an extensive variety of wildlife species. Jofie and Marina were targeting a hartebeest, but the plains were alive with a variety of different game animals. Sturdy gemsboks, with their painted faces and upright black horns, passed through the trees in the distance. In the open grasslands, great herds of springboks grazed or bedded down out of sight in the yellow grass, and kudus slipped through the shadowed game trails along the ridges and in the heaviest cover, moving, as they always did, with high anxiety.

Early on the first day, Jofie found what he was looking for—hartebeests. After tracking the herd for miles just after sunup, Jofie motioned for the hunting party to stop, and he pointed toward a grove of trees where the band of hartebeests, their long, red faces hidden in the grass, fed out in the plains, unaware of the approaching hunters. Squatting behind her son, Marina strained to see the hartebeest herd in the shade of the trees ahead of them. There was a bull among the cows, a battered old veteran with a rusty red coat and thick, knurled horns with good tips.

Jofie motioned for Marina to move forward, and they slipped around a thornbush. Marina wanted to snap a picture before she shot, so she pulled the camera she was carrying close to her and pressed the ON button. The lens opened and moved outward from the front of the camera body with a distinct mechanical hum. The hartebeests snapped to attention, craning their necks as they studied the bush before finally

Namibian thorns. (Photo courtesy of Jacques Strauss)

turning and starting off across the plains in a long-reaching gallop. The herd crested a sandy rise and vanished.

That was their only opportunity on that day to take a hartebeest, and as the sun set the plains on fire with orange light, Jofie and Marina walked back toward the truck, dusty and exhausted. Marina was not pleased at having blown her first stalk, but she took solace in one of Jofie's favorite sayings: "Every day is a hunting day, but not all days are shooting days." That would have to be enough for Marina after her first day of hunting. They returned to Rooikraal, hungry and footsore, as the first white stars appeared in the cloudless desert sky.

On her second trip afield, Marina had no intention of missing another chance at her hartebeest. As the purple light of morning began to spread across the Kalahari, Jofie and Marina set out with Joof's tracker, Johnny "Zeiss Eyes," accompanying them on the hunt. Marina carried her beloved Mannlicher rifle and looked forward to getting a chance to test her shooting skills on game.

It wasn't long before they found what they were looking for. Herds of oryxes and blue wildebeests came out onto the open plains to feed, basking in the warmth of the sun as the last crystalline drops of dew evaporated into the dry desert air. From a vantage point on a hill, the hunters watched the mixed herds feeding on the plain. A band of warthogs appeared out of the camelthorns and started rooting alongside the grazing herds. Eventually, a herd of hartebeests moved out into the open, and Jofie gave each one a good look as they filed out of the trees and onto the sunburned veld. When the last hartebeest had emerged from the trees and the herd mixed in with the other ungulates, Jofie shook his head.

There was nothing worth shooting, but the scene was quite remarkable and uniquely African. For some time, mother and son watched the herds moving and feeding together, a scene hearkening back to the days when primitive humans relied on the antelopes as food and pursued them with spears and short bows.

Jofie and Marina finally abandoned the plain where the herds blended together like awkward preteens at a school mixer. Johnny was

The outside of the main lodge at Rooikraal, home of Hunters Namibia Safaris. (Photo courtesy of Marina Lamprecht/Hunters Namibia Safaris)

waiting back at the truck, and when Jofie and Marina arrived, the group set out across the tall-grass plains under the warm winter sun. They had not gone far when Johnny waved his hand to stop Jofie. He pointed out across the plain at a band of hartebeests loafing and feeding among the bent trunks of a camelthorn forest. Jofie cut the engine and looked through his field glasses at the glossy copper-colored bodies shining on the plains like so many pennies in a fountain. There was a bull at the edge of the herd that looked as though it might be worth stalking. Jofie motioned for his mother to get her rifle, and together they set out across the dry, grassy plains.

Marina followed close behind Jofie, moving stride for stride with her son, who was almost a foot taller than she was. Marina had, after all, taught this boy to take his first steps and had held his hand and walked him through this same amber Kalahari grass when Jofie was just a child. Now he was in the lead, pointing the way and teaching his mother as she followed him. Soon they had covered almost half a mile, and all the while Jofie had kept track of the herd and traced its movements across the savanna. The hartebeests were feeding slowly to the east and Jofie moved low over the grass to intercept the rear flank of the herd. Moving close together in order not to appear as individual silhouettes, Jofie and Marina closed the distance and found the bull standing between two crooked trees, its coat contrasting shades of red with glossy black highlights at the shoulder and flank. Jofie took a moment to evaluate the hartebeest and decided that this was, indeed, the bull they wanted.

"Do you see the bull standing broadside?" Jofie asked as he propped the shooting sticks up and handed his mother her Mannlicher-Schoenauer rifle.

Marina nodded and let the rifle settle into the notch at the crest of the sticks. When the bull appeared in the center of the scope, Marina took a deep breath, held it, and pressed the trigger. The little rifle barked and rose up on the sticks with the recoil. All of the hartebeests started out across the grassy plain at full speed except for the old bull. It fell down where it had been standing and never moved again.

The old bull would have been an impressive first trophy for anyone. Marina had hunted well and had placed her shot precisely in that clutch moment when the rifle was steady and the scope centered. For her efforts, she was rewarded with a beautiful hartebeest bull, one of the world's unique and most challenging trophies. More importantly, she had taken her first animal with her son guiding her, and he had been there to share in the moment when Marina stood looking down at her fine bull.

When they returned to Rooikraal's main lodge with the hartebeest bull in the hunting car, Joof came out to share in his wife's success. Marina smiled as she addressed both her husband and her son.

"Boys, you have awakened the beast, and the game is on."

CHAPTER 15

THE OUTLIERS

Professional hunter: Vaughan Fulton
Location: Etosha

The lion may be the quintessential dangerous-game animal. Able to reach speeds of forty miles an hour and weighing over four hundred pounds, this big cat is uniquely adapted for hunting and killing. In addition, lions are often found in groups of three or more, adding multiple degrees of danger to an already deadly pursuit. Professional hunters are often unwilling to label any one member of the Big Five as the most dangerous because, obviously, any of them can and will kill you. But ask most PHs what animal they personally fear most, and you will hear the lion mentioned more than any other. Perhaps it is a primordial dread. Arguments can be made about the relative danger factor of any of the members of the Big Five, but, with the possible exception of leopards, only lions regularly killed and ate our forebears.

The modern media portrays stock-killing and man-eating lions as decrepit, moribund beasts forced to kill something other than their natural prey out of sheer desperation. With lions, as with other large predators, advanced age is only one factor that drives them to kill livestock and human beings. Many lions kill stock because it has replaced their natural food source. Others are perfectly capable of killing wild game but have learned that cattle are much easier to catch and kill than the average zebra, buffalo, or sable. Many of the rogue lions that become nuisances and even threats to farmers and villagers are young adult males forced into a life of solitude on the fringes of their former pride's range.

Such was the case when Vaughan Fulton of Fulton Classic Safaris received word that a pair of marauding male lions had established themselves on a nearby ranch. The males, likely brothers, had escaped from the confines of Etosha National Park to the north and were working their way through the ranch country. For the young male lions, the cattle on the ranches were a bounty. They were easy to kill, and without any competition from other lions, the males dedicated themselves wholly to

Returning home at the end of a hunt in the Etosha Conservancy. (Photo courtesy of Benjamin Gettinger)

killing livestock. Vaughan offered his client and friend, Sandy Trout, the rare opportunity to hunt one of the lions on a problem-animal permit, a special license offered by Namibia's MET for specific animals that have proven to be dangerous or highly destructive.

Vaughan knew that the lions were looking for an easy meal, so he set out a bait for the cats and built an elevated blind seventy yards from it. The blind was designed not only to offer maximum concealment, but also to provide a clean, clear shot without the bullet having to pass through heavy brush. In the heat of late afternoon, Vaughan and Sandy climbed into their blind, checked their rifles, and looked out at the swarm of flies that had found their bait. They waited.

Long hours passed silently as the sun peaked and started toward the western horizon, stretching the shadows out over the pale-yellow sand. In the distance, a comical-sounding go-away bird gave a nasal shriek, a sign that something was on the move. Vaughan knew it would not be long now, and just after five o'clock the two male lions

A big male lion in Etosha. (Photo courtesy of Elaine Coetzee)

moved out of cover and headed for the bait. Tails swinging, they fought over the fetid meat while the displaced flies swarmed them. Over the sound of their horrible growls, Vaughan studied the lions, trying to pick the one that his client should shoot. The government had issued only one problem-lion permit despite the fact that there were two big males. They were a matched pair, almost certainly brothers, driven by larger pride males from the fenced boundaries of Etosha into the farmland where they now held dominion.

Vaughan chose one of the males for his client and instructed Sandy to hit the cat through the shoulders. At the crack of the rifle, Sandy's lion spun and roared, lashing its tail as it ran back toward the dense thorn before Sandy could chamber another round. Running side-by-side and roaring in fury, the two males were swallowed up by the same thorns from where they had emerged moments earlier.

After the shot and the roaring escape that followed, silence fell over the winter-still plains. No breeze stirred the yellow tufts of grass or the outstretched fingers of thorn around the bait. The go-away bird was silent, and even the sociable weavers, which normally flutter atop their massive communal nests all day, were gone. Only the flies remained. They settled back on the bait and Vaughan could see their glossy blue bodies reflecting the light of late afternoon.

Vaughan and Sandy climbed out of the blind and walked toward the bait. The only sound was the crunch of the dry sand under their leather-soled hunting boots. The flies hummed and rose over the bait, blithely ignorant of the goings-on all around them. They only cared about what was dead and what was not.

Near the bait, the sand was disturbed where the big male had spun as the bullet hit him. The great pug marks, almost nine inches wide, were spread at great length where the lions had run back across the clearing and into the thorns. Light was fading. It was potentially lethal to follow up wounded lions in thornbush scrub at any hour of the day, but to move in after two lions at daylight's last purple ebb was beyond foolhardy—it was suicide. After a short tracking job that led into even thicker thornbush, Vaughan called off the hunt until morning.

In the darkness, the lions moved through the narrow game trails within the labyrinth of thorn. Sometime in the night, the two males split up, the wounded lion moving off to the right to lie down while its brother continued on, moving deeper into ranch country and vanishing under the faint blue moonbeams that filtered through the acacia limbs and settled on the sand like the shattered pieces of dull white glass. The wounded cat held tight, licking its wounds and building its reserves until the sun rose up over the smooth brown hills.

At dawn, Vaughan, Sandy, and two of Vaughan's Herero trackers found the lions' spoor and set out after them, moving slowly through the network of trails cut through the morass of black hookthorn. As the trackers moved through the head-high thorn, Vaughan covered the trail with his open-sighted .458, focusing his attention and waiting for any sign of the lions ahead. Suddenly Vaughan's trackers stopped and pointed down both lanes of a bifurcated game trail. The lions had separated.

As there was no blood to indicate which lion was hit, the decision was made to remain on the main trail. After half an hour, though, the trackers shook their heads, turned, and indicated to Vaughan that the lion they were following was not the wounded one. The men decided they would have to backtrack to get back to the point where the lions had separated. The hunters returned to the split in the trail and turned onto the other track, certain now that at the end of this trail they would find the wounded cat. In such thick cover the lion could be anywhere, and there was no hope of seeing the cat before the men were well within range of a charge. The hunt had taken a deadly turn, and it was only a matter of time before the lion made its final stand.

Half a mile down the trail, the trackers stopped and froze as if they were cast in steel. Vaughan's gaze followed the trail thirty yards ahead to where the lion lay stretched out in the shade of a camelthorn tree. Vaughan's men studied the cat for a few seconds before turning and indicating that this was definitely the correct male, the one Sandy had wounded the night before. The lion was resting with its head turned away from the men, and Vaughan gave Sandy the command to shoot. Although no words passed between the men, Sandy could read Vaughan's eyes.

Make it count.

Sandy shouldered his rifle, and when the iron sights fell on the lion's shoulder, he pressed the trigger. The cat was up at once, twisting in midair like a hooked marlin. In two bounds it covered half the ground between itself and the men, making a series of coughing grunts. Vaughan squared his .458 below the lion's chin and pressed the trigger, giving the cat a 500-grain thumping square in the chest that might have derailed a locomotive. But it wasn't enough to stop the lion's onslaught. As Vaughan started to work his bolt—with the cat twenty feet away and closing—he tripped and fell backward over an errant clump of thorn, dropping into the desert sand.

The shot had slowed the cat enough that Sandy had time to rack another cartridge into the chamber. From less than an arm's length, he belted the lion with another shot just behind the front shoulder, driving the cat off Vaughan. It turned immediately and came for Sandy, its rapier claws outstretched as it reached out for the hunter's head with its jaws, trying for the neck bite that would end Sandy's hunting career and his life.

Out of cartridges, Sandy had nothing to defend himself with except the empty rifle clutched in his hands. Stepping back to avoid the lion's rush, he too had fallen and was now staring up into the blazing yellow eyes of the lion as it opened its jaws and rushed in for the kill. With astounding presence of mind, Sandy knew his only hope was to drive his rifle into the cat's mouth. The pain of the lion's teeth entering his skin was lost in the wave of adrenaline that now surged over Sandy as he thrust the fore-end of his rifle into the cat's jaws, shattering one of the lion's teeth and stunning the cat.

When the lion pulled back, Sandy felt the rifle being tugged out of his hands—the cat had placed its foot through the sling and was now pulling the rifle farther from Sandy with each step. With renewed fervor, the lion came again, driving in to finally kill the man, when it was finally derailed by two-and-a-half tons of muzzle blast from Vaughan's .458 at point-blank range. The lion dropped like a demolished bridge across Sandy's legs.

As the shot echoed, the two men scrambled away from the lion, which lay outstretched in a column of rising dust. Sandy saw that his hand was bleeding, but at least it was still there. No fingers were missing, no bones splintered. They had survived. Together Vaughan and Sandy had made it through one of the most terrifying encounters in all of hunting—a charge by a wounded lion. For Vaughan and Sandy, the experience brought home the truth about dangerous-game hunting: At any moment, the odds can change.

CHAPTER 16

THE DAYDREAM KUDU

Professional Hunter: Jacques Strauss
Location: Central Highlands

For Jacques Strauss, the red sands of the Kalahari served as his childhood sandbox, and the vast open savannas and rolling dunes were his backyard. From boyhood, Jacques had helped his parents, Danie and Ansie, manage Kowas Hunting Safaris in the heart of the Dorbabis Conservancy, an hour's drive east of the international airport in Windhoek. Growing up on a hunting ranch in the Kalahari as he did, Jacques developed the skills necessary to operate the camp. He learned to recognize the various tracks of the Kalahari's many antelopes, and he could identify the birds that surrounded the lodge by their songs alone. He could track wounded game, direct a skinning crew, fix blown tires and broken rifles, and keep clients entertained and happy during their time at Kowas. By the light of the evening campfires, Jacques heard stories from hunters who had traveled to Namibia from around the world in search of game.

But there are certain lessons that even a childhood spent living in the Kalahari cannot teach. This meant that, despite his desire to spend every day helping at the ranch, Jacques was forced to attend a private school. While there, Jacques could never offer his full attention to his studies, and he often dreamed of going into the bush in search of game. Like so many hunters around the world, the trophy Jacques most desired was a magnificent kudu bull. He had watched clients take kudus, and for years had often seen the hunting car pull in with a big bull in the back—the great twisting horns, colored like a well-aged walnut rifle stock, sticking out of the truck bed. Jacques understood the desire of hunters who came from every corner of the earth to find a really good kudu bull.

During the months leading up to the hunting season, Jacques and his friend Friedrich set about planning a kudu hunt. The two eighteen-year-olds decided that they would pack their gear into the rocky hills surrounding Friedrich's home on Saint Elmo Ranch in the foothills of the Central Plateau, at the western edge of the Kalahari. Over and over again, the boys checked their lists of gear, adding items here and there as they tried to visualize the stalk and the shot. The days seemed to pass slowly, and the boys could think of little else besides the end of the school year and setting out into the wild in search of one of the world's greatest trophies.

Jacques's and Friedrich's kudu hunt would not be based in a lodge. They would not enjoy a comfortable bed after the day's hunt or a warm meal waiting when they returned from the field. Instead, the boys gathered the goods they needed to set up camp high in the rocky hills that overlooked Saint Elmo ranch. They set out on the evening before their hunt, both of them loaded down with the accoutrements of a hunting camp, including tent, bedrolls, extra clothing, and Jacques's prized 7x64 Brenneke rifle. The boys set out in the fading evening light in search of a place to make camp, looking very much like a classic African hunting party except that they were the only porters.

When the sun set behind the rocky hills and the first stars flitted dimly above the peaks, Jacques and Friedrich were still struggling to negotiate the rocks and find a suitable place for their camp. Experience would have taught the boys that despite months of anticipation, it would have been a better idea to wait until the following morning to set up their camp. The difficulties they faced while trying to set up camp in the darkness were compounded by the heavy packs they wore and the fact that the boys had brought only a single dim flashlight to guide them over the tumbled rocks.

After an hour spent following the small yellow beam, they found a place high among the granite cliffs and established their camp, stumbling in the darkness as they organized their possessions. When the two boys finally lay in their tent listening to the chorus of animal sounds that are to the African night what traffic noises are to the world's largest metropolitan centers, they dreamed of their quest for

Glassing for game in the Kalahari. (Photo courtesy of Jacques Strauss)

the king of all antelopes. As the boys drifted off, the fat yellow moon started its long climb into the night sky.

It was not the usual chatter of starlings and go-away birds that woke the boys the next day. Instead, a drumming rain battered the small tent. The downpour soon overwhelmed the small canvas tent and drenched all the gear the boys had brought along for the hunt. In all their months of planning and preparation, Jacques and Friedrich had not counted on rain, but throughout the morning the heavens continued the onslaught. Soaked and shivering in the damp confines of the tent, Jacques considered giving up the quest for kudu in exchange for a hot shower and hours of sleep in a real bed without granite for a mattress and a misshapen boulder for a pillow. But the rain ebbed and soon the deluge ceased, leaving the boys wet and cold but not without hope that somehow they could still manage to find a big kudu bull in the rocky canyons.

Each boy had a different idea about what the next move should be. As the last thunder bellowed in the distance, a rift developed that threatened to end the hunt. Jacques wanted to hunt from the rocky ridge tops, glassing the canyons for bulls escaping the rain, while Friedrich suggested they stay low and stalk through heavy cover at the base of the hills. Like the rain, the disagreement passed, and the boys decided to climb up to the top of the mountain and glass into the surrounding valleys.

The ascent was difficult. The smooth, round faces of the rocks were difficult to negotiate at the best of times. After a rain, the route was treacherous, and any misplaced step could result in something worse than a blown opportunity for a kudu. Finally, however, the boys made it to the top and settled into the gray rocks to glass the shadowy canyons that stretched out in different directions like the legs of a spider.

There were kudus in the valleys, but no mature bulls and certainly nothing that warranted a harrowing stalk through the rocks. Oryxes were abundant. Virtually every open patch of grassy plain that the boys could see had at least one oryx feeding somewhere on it. The oryxes, which were far more accustomed to the heat of the desert than to heavy rains, looked wet and bedraggled as they fed out into the open areas surrounding the hills, their parchment-colored coats matted by the water.

Jacques and Friedrich continued along the ridge top, stopping to glass each dark crevasse below them for kudus. The storm had passed, but gray clouds still lingered over the highlands. The boys could hear rushing water making its way down the mountainside as the dry creek beds swelled with murky runoff. Jacques had all but given up on ever finding a kudu bull and had almost resigned himself to going back to collect his gear and head for home when he felt Friedrich's fingers drumming on his shoulder.

Jacques followed his friend's outstretched finger to a brushy slope on the opposite ridge more than four hundred yards away. There, feeding through the rain-darkened thornbush, was a magnificent kudu bull with wide horns and deep, heavy curls. They watched the bull as it fed out into the clearing. The old kudu stopped occasionally and lifted its great head into the air, rotating its wide ears while it studied each shadow and rock cleft. The bull moved farther out of the thorns into the clearing, slipping through the open country with the hesitation and anxiety that is a hallmark of the species. The bull's shoulder was taller than Jacques's head, and even if he could have touched the great horns, it would have been all Jacques could have done to stretch his fingertips from one ivory tip to the next.

There were several challenges facing the boys if they hoped to get within range of Jacques's 7x64 rifle. First, there was a lot of ground to cover between their current position and the opposite slope. They would have to cover that ground without alerting the bull, which was moving slowly out of sight and even farther out of range as the boys dithered on how best to intercept it. The ground was wet, which would make it easier to stalk silently, but maneuvering over the wet ground would be a trick. One slip on a loose stone would send the bull bounding back into the thorns. To make matters worse, a single oryx bull was feeding just below the kudu on the ridge. If they were to have any chance for a shot, the boys had to approach both the kudu and the oryx without being noticed.

The kudu wasn't going to stay in the open very long, and Jacques knew if they didn't get moving now they might not have time to cover the ground. The boys started down the slope, staying low to the glossy red-and-brown rocks. Every few paces, Jacques checked on the bull, which began to feed alongside the oryx higher on the slope. During the descent, the boys kept an eye on both the oryx and the kudu, stopping when one or both of the animals stopped feeding, and moving again when both the oryx and kudu lowered their heads. The boys moved from one large rock to the next for cover, careful not to be caught in the open. The last portion of the hillside was particularly challenging as it was very open, broken only by small, scattered rocks and wet tufts of yellow grass growing from the ground like so many mangy, upturned broom heads.

From the bottom, as Jacques and Friedrich watched the two bulls feeding in and out of the patchwork of brown thorns on the otherwise

Jacques and his friend resting by the campfire while on safari. (Photo courtesy of Jacques Strauss)

amber-colored slope, Jacques decided they should start their uphill stalk at an angle so that a large tree would shield them from the kudu. They would still have to contend with the oryx. With Jacques in the lead, the two boys started up the hillside, pressing themselves down onto the rocky earth whenever the oryx bull lifted its head.

After two hours, the difficulty of the stalk had whittled away even Jacques's enthusiasm. His face and belly had been pressed against the wet, rocky ground the whole time, and each time the oryx bull looked up, Jacques had to flatten himself, breathing the wet, soggy smell of the saturated earth just below his chin. Whenever the oryx stopped feeding and spent several minutes scanning the hillside, Jacques was forced to press himself even farther into the earth, feeling every rock and errant thorn along the length of his soaked frame. Whenever the oryx finally lowered its head, Jacques would scramble to cover the next few yards.

Jacques had to cover the last ten yards alone because there was no cover left between the hunter and his quarry. If both boys tried to close the gap, the odds were they would be seen, so Friedrich held back to stay out of the kudu's line of sight. Just before Jacques started across the last patch of open ground, he looked back at his friend. No words passed between them, but like all hunters, they had learned to communicate without words when necessary. This was it. The months of planning and preparation had come down to this last thirty feet of open ground.

Jacques edged across the slope and looked up at the open place on the hillside where the kudu should have been. He saw nothing. The wet, brown earth was completely empty. Jacques was astounded. Surely if the kudu had been alarmed, they would have seen a reaction from the oryx bull. The oryx, however, had not stopped grazing. It continued working its way through the rocks, looking unconcerned and unalarmed.

But where was the kudu?

Long moments passed as Jacques, lying flat on the wet earth like a stalking leopard, slowly lifted his head higher above the rocks as he scanned the slope above for the kudu. The oryx remained where it was and gave no indication that the kudu had sensed its pursuers. It was possible that the old kudu had simply fed out of sight through the clumps of wait-a-bit thorn. Jacques blinked the sweat from his eyes. His dark hair was soaked and clung to his head like seaweed washed ashore during high tide and left behind as the water receded. Long moments passed while the oryx continued feeding, oblivious to the hunter who lay prone on the rocks just below it. Jacques scanned the slope from bush to bush, trying to look through the tangled branches to spot the oblong curve of the kudu's ear or the walnut-and-ivory tip of a horn passing over brush.

Jacques fixed his gaze on something that, although he did not recognize it at first, was out of place among the branches and wet rocks. Soon he saw movement and realized it was the kudu's nose. It was tempting for Jacques to stand up and take his chance at the

Kudu camp in the Kalahari. (Photo courtesy of Jacques Strauss)

bull, but instead, he waited. Jacques knew better than to rush the shot by rising up too soon and alerting the kudu. Eventually the bull stepped out, as magnificent as ever, and began weaving through the thorn scrub just up the slope from where Jacques lay pressed against the rocks.

Inch by agonizing inch, Jacques crawled forward toward a broken tree ten yards ahead of him. Halfway there, a rock rolled from under his knee, clacking its way down the slope and drawing the kudu's attention immediately toward Jacques, who lay exposed between two patches of cover. The bull turned and gave the characteristic sharp bark that meant it would not remain on the hillside much longer.

Jacques knew it was the only chance he would have for a shot at the bull. As the kudu turned, Jacques scrambled to his feet and made for the broken tree stump to his right. He dropped his rifle against the soft, pulpy wood and pressed his face against the stock. The kudu was moving uphill and would soon be swallowed by heavy cover. Unless his shot was quick and true, the image of the bull disappearing in the lens of the scope would be Jacques's last view of his lost trophy.

As the bull started toward the heavy thorn, its wide horns swinging over the top of its head, Jacques found the bull through the scope and felt the cold, metallic curve of the trigger. Taking one last breath, Jacques blinked the sweat from his eyes, settled the cross hairs on the leading edge of the bull's chest, and squeezed when the rifle came steady.

The report echoed among the columns of gray stone as the kudu lurched forward, moving in full flight up the hill toward a patch of cover. Jacques leaped to his feet, throwing the bolt as he moved over the rocks toward higher ground. Unable to get a clear view of the kudu, Jacques scrambled back beside Friedrich, who had remained among the rain-soaked boulders at the base of the hill. From there they had a clear view of the retreating bull. Steadying his rifle on his friend's shoulder, Jacques readied himself for what would be his last chance at the bull.

Jacques and the kudu he worked so hard for. (Photo courtesy of Jacques Strauss)

The kudu was three hundred yards away and moving uphill. The only chance Jacques had to bring the bull down was to take a raking shot through the pelvis and up into the vitals. Accounting for the range and estimating the holdover while steadying the rifle on Friedrich's shoulder, Jacques found his target through the scope, held just over his desired point of impact, and pressed the trigger. The 170-grain bullet caught the kudu in the rear ham and drove up through the chest cavity. The bull took a step, stumbled, and fell down at the edge of the thicket. One more shot finished it.

Friedrich gave his friend a congratulatory backslap and together the boys ran up the hill. Scrambling over the loose rocks and weaving through the thorn, the boys finally came upon the kudu bull, its dark eyes wide and still as it lay outstretched. They touched the wispy mane, the delicate-looking legs, the smooth gray hide, and the pencil-thin white lines that ran down both sides of the magnificent bull's body. They touched the horns. The tips were a creamy yellow color that turned abruptly to a deep, walnut brown. They ran their fingers around the wide outside curl of the horns.

They had done it. The hunt had been a success, and all their months of daydreaming and preparation had been rewarded. But the work was far from over. They were high in the mountains and miles from any two-track road. The only way to get the bull out was to quarter it and pack it through the rocky hills to the road below. It was hard work even for two strong boys of eighteen. They started down the hill and climbed the next ridge, struggling under the strain of the meat they carried on their backs. Eventually, twelve hours after the hunt began, the hunters and their bull were back at Saint Elmo Ranch.

After a round of congratulations from the farm hands, Jacques put a tape on his bull's horns, which measured 56 inches around the curve. The bull itself weighed more than 800 pounds. Jacques and Friedrich had taken their bull honestly, on foot, in the bull's territory. It was a fine story and a fine start to the hunting careers of two young Namibian men.

Even though it was Jacques who had pulled the trigger, the excitement of the chase and the memory of pursuing the bull was something that both boys would share for the rest of their lives.

With the kudu meat hanging in the meat locker and the magnificent head salted and caped in the trophy shed, Jacques and Friedrich dried themselves from the rain and rested after the long day's hunt.

Jacques Strauss would later go on to finish school and be certified among the ranks of Namibia's professional hunters. He now works at Kowas Safaris, guiding other hunters on their quest for Africa's gray ghost and a variety of other plains game on Kowas Farm at the western edge of the vast Kalahari.

CHAPTER 17

CORNERED

Professional hunter: Karl Stumpfe
Location: Windhoek

"*Jagluiperd!*"

Karl Stumpfe shifted the hunting car into neutral and looked over the thornbush on the left and right side of the road. The cook in the front seat repeated "*jagluiperd,*" the Afrikaans word for cheetah. (Translated literally, it means "hunting leopard.") Karl shifted the car into reverse and began backing over the red sand toward the place where the cook said he had seen a large cheetah sitting beside the road. Moving slowly so as not to stir up any more dust than they already had, Karl backed the car up to the place where the cook insisted he had seen the cat. Words passed between the cook and one of Karl's trackers sitting in the front seat. From the rear, Karl's client asked what the commotion was about.

"He says he saw a cheetah," Karl said as he continued looking into the winter-dry forest of dingy brown thornbushes powdered with the dust of a hundred passing vehicles. The interwoven mat of thorns made good cover for any game hidden at the edge of the winding road.

Karl, owner of Ndumo Safaris, and his client had started their safari in northern Namibia, hunting elephants at Karl's camp in the Caprivi Strip. They had enjoyed tremendous luck, and Karl's client, an American doctor, had taken a magnificent bull early in the hunt. Only a couple days into the safari and with an elephant already in the salt, Karl and his client decided to head to Karl's plains-game hunting area, less than an hour's drive from the capital city of Windhoek.

The dry, rolling hills of the Central Plateau were far different from the swamps and mopane forests of Caprivi, but there was a wide variety of plains game on license at Karl's camp. His client had enjoyed several successful days of hunting, and today he had to leave for home. Seeing a wild cheetah on the way to the airport would have been the perfect end to a magnificent Namibian safari.

Karl scanned the thornbush behind them, straining to see between the outstretched branches and ivory-colored thorns. If the cheetah was in the thick bush, it would almost certainly have to move for Karl to see it. With the car idling, the men watched for any sign of the cat. Karl trusted the eyes of his camp staff, but it seemed that, at least this time, his cook had been mistaken.

"Leopard!" Karl's client shouted from the backseat. By the time Karl turned, there was nothing in the road. His client insisted that he had seen a leopard running at full speed across the road directly in front of the hunting car. Karl pulled to the side of the sand road and killed the engine. The men stepped out of the car and started down the road on foot, pausing now and then to look for spoor in the warm, clay-colored sand at the side of the road. Talking quietly and moving in single file, the men approached the place where the client said the leopard had crossed. Karl hoped they would find a track, and if they were really fortunate they might even catch a glimpse of the elusive cat slipping through the maze of thorns along the side of the road.

Karl stopped suddenly and motioned for the others to halt. There, hidden in the dry brown web of thorns on the right side of the road, was the leopard. The cat pressed itself flat under the canopy of a low-growing acacia and watched the men, who were only twenty-five yards away, through a veil of dried grass as its tail moved left and right. It was a young female about the size of a collie, and it was lying perfectly flat against the shadowed sand with its head low, watching the men through wide, yellow-green eyes.

One of the trackers started to move ahead in the road, passing the cat and starting in toward it for a better look.

"Don't go any farther," Karl ordered. "She'll feel that she's been cornered and we'll have a problem. We need to get back in the car."

The tracker took another half a step and strained to see through the thorns, apparently unwilling to leave the place without getting a good look at the cat. Karl's client snapped a photo. Karl spoke to his tracker again, this time telling him plainly that they had pushed their

A leopard in the shadows of dense cover. (Photo courtesy of Jofie Lamprecht)

luck as far as they should. It was time to get back to the vehicle and leave the cat alone.

Karl's tracker seemed transfixed by the cat, but finally he heeded Karl's warning and started to back away. It was too late. The leopard came boiling out of the dry grass with a furious burst of grunts, exploding from its shadowy refuge under the thorn tree and appearing as a glistening golden streak that bore down on the men with tail-lashing fury. When the cat came, the group of men turned with a single scream and ran wildly back toward the hunting car—all of them but Karl, who stood still and tried to turn the cat with a series of shouts. Karl believed that once the cat felt free of the oncoming men, it would shear off its course and turn back toward cover. He stood his ground and shouted loudly, hoping to turn the cat or at least give the rest of the crew time to get back to the car.

The leopard continued directly toward him, covering the ground in a series of rapid strides. Karl thought of looking on the ground for a rock or a stick, but he knew better than to take his eye off the oncoming cat. When the leopard was almost upon him, Karl pulled back his leg and kicked as hard as he could, swinging his boot at the head of the oncoming cat.

In a flash, the leopard grabbed his thigh with both forelegs, the hooked white claws cutting deep into Karl's leg as the cat turned its head and bit down into the flesh at the junction of Karl's hamstring and buttocks. With a shout of pain, Karl tried to fight off the furious leopard. The leopard and the man crashed down into the sand, Karl on top of the cat, which continued to try to gut him with its rear claws.

Fortunately for Karl, the leopard had fallen with its left rear leg pinned under its body, and Karl reached with his right hand to try to grab the cat's right foot before it could do any serious damage. After a series of misses and lacerations from the claws, Karl managed to grab the cat's right rear leg. With his forearm against the cat's neck, he began to press his weight down onto the enraged leopard as it twisted and snarled beneath him. Karl managed to pin the cat down and tried desperately

Karl, his client, and a big leopard. (Photo courtesy of Karl Stumpfe)

to cut off its air supply while trying to keep away from the claws and fangs that had already done considerable damage to his body.

As he fought to keep his hold and avoid any further injuries, Karl heard a shout from the vehicle. "Did you catch it?"

Out of breath and bleeding from scores of wounds, Karl shouted back, "Yes! Come and help me!"

Karl's cook and tracker steeled their nerves and started toward where their employer lay stretched out at full length atop the enraged leopard. Karl was bleeding badly and needed help, but the most important task—dispatching the leopard—remained unfinished. With the tracker holding the cat's head down, Karl took a knife and finally ended the struggle.

In the few seconds that Karl had wrestled with the cat, he had sustained an assemblage of cuts, both superficial and deep, to his hands, legs, thighs, and buttocks. At the side of the road, not far from where the leopard lay dead, Karl's client took the emergency kit and treated the twenty-seven wounds that the cat had inflicted with its fangs and claws. At the hospital, Karl had to undergo a series of tetanus shots and the first of a series of rabies shots. He was also given strong doses of antibiotics since a bite or scratch from a cat always carries the risk of turning septic.

With his cuts treated and his client safely on his way home after a grand safari, Karl had some time to recuperate and think about what he might have done differently. First, he decided that he should always carry a firearm when dealing with dangerous game, and, second, he instructed his staff regarding how they should react during conflicts with cats. It was lucky they had had an emergency kit on hand, but the kit would have to be restocked since his doctor-client had used most of the gauze and antibiotic cream to clean Karl's wounds. Most of all, Karl hoped he would never be involved in another incident like the one he had just lived through. Wrestling with leopards, Karl decided, is an unpleasant pastime.

CHAPTER 18

The Floodwater Tusker

Professional hunter: Jofie Lamprecht
Location: Caprivi

The Kwando River, the lifeline of the Caprivi and the source of the region's abundant water, had swollen beyond the limits of its banks and spilled out into the surrounding areas, rolling thick and brown over the papyrus-choked flood plains of the Caprivi Strip. The grasslands around the river were inundated by the flow, and as the volume of water increased, only the highest points of land remained above the river like islands rising from a boiling, frothy sea. The normally green plains were a shimmering ocean punctuated by oases of trees and tall grass. The high water would make elephant hunting—never an easy task, anyway—all the more difficult.

The problems associated with the high water were compounded, ironically enough, by seasonal fires that swept over any patch of land that was not under water. Between the flooding and the fires, it seemed American Karl Pedroni's safari with Jofie Lamprecht would be a total loss. But such was not the case. Jofie had already guided his seventy-five-year-old client to an old buffalo bull with a heavy boss and an outstanding hippo. Leopard hunting was not going as planned, as is so often the case; the big tom that had been consistently hitting a bait staunchly refused to show itself during daylight hours.

Elephant hunting wasn't going so well for Jofie and his client, either. On day eighteen of the three-week safari, Jofie sensed that Karl was beginning to doubt that he would get his chance at one of the big bulls that haunt the jungles of thorn and reeds in the Kwando region. Perhaps even Jofie had his doubts about finding a big bull under these conditions. In any other year it would have been much simpler to find the elephants, which rely on the Kwando's year-round water supply and will come to drink every night. Had the elephants been coming to water, Jofie might have known where to find their spoor; then, after evaluating the tracks, the group could set out to catch the elephants.

Elephant herd drinking in Caprivi Strip. (Photo courtesy of Jofie Lamprecht)

But the swollen river meant that the need to drink was not so urgent, so the elephants were scattered among the green riverine forests, hidden in a veil of ash and smoke.

Jofie was intent on finding a bull despite the rotten conditions, and he climbed into the Land Cruiser on the eighteenth day of the safari showing the same resolve that he had when Karl had stepped onto the tarmac at the airport almost three weeks earlier. The elephants were there, Jofie knew, hidden within a labyrinth of flooded forests and scattered islands. In addition, this was to be Karl's first elephant—the pinnacle of his hunting career and the game animal he most desired. It also happened to be Jofie's first Namibian elephant, too. He had hunted for several elephants in Tanzania as part of his big-game apprenticeship, but he had never guided an elephant hunter by himself.

The hunting party set out in the Land Cruiser, moving south along a two-track road through the haze of the fire and the shimmering water that stood in scattered puddles after the latest rain. Jofie made his way slowly through the tangled green forests of the Kwando, keeping a close eye out for any patch of gray or muddy brown hide that would betray an elephant's presence among the towering makalani palm trees. The hunters continued driving south among the dense green forests until they reached the boundary of the hunting area and the edge of Kwando National Park. Jofie stopped the Cruiser at the edge of the park and looked down almost in disbelief at the wide, round tracks that indicated a lone elephant bull had left the park and moved into the hunting area.

The tracks were still fresh. The massive prints still had sharp edges, so Jofie knew the elephant had passed this way not long before. Although he could tell nothing about the bull's ivory from the track, it was a very large print and was certainly the most encouraging bit of elephant sign the men had seen so far in the grime and haze of the smoky landscape. It was certainly worth having a look at the bull to see if its teeth were as substantial as its footprint. Jofie waved the men down from the truck.

Karl stepped down from the Cruiser, rifle in hand, and he and the rest of the men moved into the recently burned brush. Here, farther inland from the river, there was less water and the ground was dry enough for good tracking. It was even dry enough that a carelessly placed boot had the potential to grind dry leaves into the soil and alert the bull to the presence of the hunters. They would have to be careful not to spook the bull before they got in range for a look at its ivory. The dense grass and thorn meant that the bull could be close-by, concealed by a veil of heavy foliage.

The elephant was moving quickly through the heavy cover. The hunters had been following the bull's spoor for miles when Jofie's lead

Jofie and his client with a very big, old Caprivi bull. (Photo courtesy of Jofie Lamprecht)

tracker stopped the party with an outstretched arm. There, moving and feeding across an open patch of ground, was the elephant. Its deeply sunken temples, thick trunk, and sagging belly told Jofie that it was an old, solitary bull that was past its breeding prime and a perfect bull to harvest. Its right-side tusk was broken off short but was very thick, like the tusks of most Caprivi bulls, and it was stained with the sap and dust of years in the heavy bush. Jofie couldn't see the other tusk, but judging by the two feet of thick, stained ivory that showed on the bull's right side, the old elephant was a good trophy.

The bull turned slightly left, spreading its wide, venous ears and gently bringing them back against its body. Humphrey, Jofie's tracker, slapped his thigh and squeezed it with both hands to signal to Jofie that the bull's ivory was very thick. That was all that Jofie needed to see. If his seasoned tracker had caught a glimpse of the far-side ivory and believed that it was good, then this was just the type of elephant Karl had traveled thousands of miles in search of.

"Karl, this is your bull."

They watched the old elephant feed in the stillness of the late afternoon. The sun was slipping slowly down toward the tops of the palms, and the elephant cast a great shadow that stretched far behind it over the grassy plain. The bull was too far away to shoot, and there was very little cover between the elephant and the hunters. Jofie knew if he and Karl lost their chance to take this old bull, they might not find its equal on this safari.

The only piece of cover between the men and the elephant was the tall, gray finger of a termite mound. The heap of earth rose up like a crooked fang directly between the hunters and the old bull that was moving slowly across the open ground toward heavy cover on the opposite side of the clearing. Reaching the termite mound meant covering a lot of open ground; there was no vegetation to break up the outline of the hunters if the bull heard a slight sound or suddenly decided to turn around. The wind was good, however; a gentle breeze was pushing against Jofie's face as he tried to weigh all of the variables quickly and decide whether to try to reach the termite mound. One broken branch or the clank of a rifle barrel against a wristwatch might spell disaster.

The men dumped all unnecessary equipment and started for the termite mound in single file. It was impossible to move over the dry, burned-out earth without making any noise, but with each step, the hunters closed the gap a bit more, continuing until they were almost within the bull's shadow. The elephant continued feeding, its tail waving gently as the men watched the bull's great bulk moving slowly among a cluster of tall trees, now only a dozen yards ahead of the hunters.

As Jofie leaned forward to have a look around the mound, he heard a moaning whine and then a sharp pop like the report of a rifle. He saw the bull's great, gray head resting squarely against the heavy trunk of a knob-thorn tree. The bull leaned against the tree, pushing its many tons into the trunk. With each push, the elephant was shaking dry leaves from the crown as the tree cracked and shuddered under the force of the old bull's mass. The elephant's enormous strength caused the tree to quiver and sway farther and farther until there was a sudden violent crack like a thunderclap, and the great knob-thorn tree, which had been in Caprivi as long as the old bull itself, toppled and crashed within yards of the termite mound. The uppermost branches fell in a cloud of dust directly ahead of the men.

The bull stood beside the fallen tree and slowly plucked the blossoms from the toppled boughs. But the tree had fallen so close to the termite mound that it effectively blocked any shot from that side. The scent of the uprooted tree drifted past the men, a sweet odor that blended with the pungent aroma of the old bull itself. As the men listened to the soft sound of the bull feeding on the flowers, Jofie motioned Karl around to the left side of the termite mound.

They moved at a crawl, careful not to misstep and alarm the bull. When Karl and Jofie rounded the opposite side of the mound, they could see the elephant's gray, wrinkled hip. They had no shot, and now there was nothing to do but wait and hope that the bull would offer a better

The local residents gather and begin the skinning process. The bull provided much-needed protein to nearby families. (Photo courtesy of Jofie Lamprecht)

target. Besides, Jofie hadn't yet had a look at the left-side ivory, and he wanted to see it himself before he gave the go-ahead.

After some time, the bull casually circled to the left, its great ears slapping gently against its knobby head. The left tusk was as thick as the right and a full two feet longer, making the old elephant an exceptional trophy. Karl slipped into position, and Jofie tried to indicate to him the angle and correct placement of the shot. Jofie and Karl slowly rose, standing not more than fifty feet from the bull. Karl took aim, resting his rifle on the termite mound for the shot.

At the crack of the rifle, the bull turned and thundered for the scant cover of the forest, toppling within twenty yards like a great building collapsing under a demolition charge. When the dust settled and the men walked forward, they saw their bull stretched out on the dry, open ground, its longest tusk—stained, scarred, and as thick as a man's leg—rising up in a crescent from its wrinkled head.

The largest tusk on Karl's bull weighed eighty pounds and measured more than six feet in length. Caprivi elephants tend to have short, heavy ivory, and Karl's bull is a tremendous trophy. (Photo courtesy of Jofie Lamprecht)

Jofie's men began the work of removing the great tusks from their sockets. The shorter, working tusk measured 4½ feet long and weighed 55 pounds. The greater tusk was more than 6 feet in length and weighed 80 pounds. Jofie slapped his client on the back and congratulated him on a very fine first elephant. For Jofie, it was a fine first bull as well.

CHAPTER 19

THE TRIPLE THREAT

Professional hunter: Gunter Schwalm
Location: Central Highlands

Jacek Papaj sat beside the *braai* at the remote Oryx Camp of Omalanga Safaris in Namibia's central highlands, marveling at the stars that seemed to crowd every inch of the night sky. It had been a fantastic safari so far for Jacek. The Polish hunter had already taken a variety of plains game, including a magnificent sable bull, the trophy he most desired. The hunt for the old black bull with the arching, heavily ridged horns had been challenging. Jacek sat back and looked over at the dim outline of the trophy shed where the bull's cape was salted and spread in preparation for shipping to Windhoek and on to Europe. Taking the old bull had been a longtime dream of Jacek's. The success was bittersweet, though, since the growing collection of trophies Jacek had added to the shed meant that his hunt was quickly coming to an end.

Jacek's professional hunter, Gunter Schwalm, sat down beside his client. In the light of the fire, Jacek saw the intensity on Schwalm's face.

"You have a once-in-a-lifetime opportunity," Schwalm said. Jacek leaned forward to listen as Gunter continued. "Not far from Oryx Camp, reports have filtered into the Namibian Ministry of Environment and Tourism about a large male lion that escaped from the boundaries of Etosha National Park and is working its way south through the game farms and cattle ranches of the central highlands, killing stock and terrorizing villagers and farmers along the way. It appears that the lion has also tried its luck on humans; although reports are unverified, the lion may have been responsible for the deaths of two missing people on a farm not far from Outjo. So, Jacek, are you interested in going after this cat?"

Namibia's MET has the authority to declare any animal that poses a significant risk to human life or livestock a "problem" animal. Such a declaration makes it legal to take that animal and export it, provided it is not one of the species that is controlled by international law under

Namibia's lions are among the largest in all of Africa. (Photo courtesy of Jacques Strauss)

CITES. Problem-animal permits are rare (in large part to prevent unscrupulous parties from baiting animals out of national parks), but they can provide a fortunate hunter with a once-in-a-lifetime opportunity to take a trophy that would not otherwise be available. In addition, hunting clients taking problem animals provide much-needed revenue to communities that bear the financial burden of conflicts with troublesome animals.

Jacek had been presented with a rare opportunity to hunt one of Africa's classic big-game species. He had never hunted any type of dangerous game, and suddenly he found himself faced with the opportunity to track down a potential man-eater in the thick wait-a-bit thorns of the Namibian highlands. The decision was not one to be taken lightly, just as the task was not one to be undertaken halfheartedly.

"When and where do we hunt this lion?" Jacek asked.

"In my opinion, it must be on one of the neighboring farms," Gunter answered. "Most of the trouble has been nearby. The farmer beside us keeps a lioness as a pet, and she's in heat now. I think the lion is in the area because of her, and he will probably remain close-by while she is in estrous."

There was little time to make a decision. It was impossible to say how long the lion would stay in the area, if it had not already left. Many of the lions escaping Etosha are young males that have been pushed out of their maternal pride, or older lions that have been driven from their positions as breeding males by younger cats. These nomadic lions search out new territories and often resort to killing stock. Gunter believed, based on the reports from nearby farmers who had seen evidence of the cat, that it was a young male. Now the onus was on Jacek Papaj to decide whether he wanted to hunt the lion or not.

He agreed.

Gunter and Jacek set out the next afternoon for a nearby farm where the lion had been heard roaring. The owner had both a female lion and an old male that he kept in a pen under special permission from the Namibian government. The lioness was, as Gunter had heard, in heat.

When Gunter and Jacek arrived at the farm, which sat on a tall hill overlooking the broken plains and scattered rock kopjes of the central plateau, the landowner mentioned that he had found a freshly killed kudu cow in some heavy brush not far from the pen where the lion and lioness were kept. The remains of the cow indicated that the lion had killed it the night before, but tracking was going to be impossible in the heavy bush. The men went down from the main lodge to the brush not far from the pen where the old lion and lioness were kept. Although there were no tracks visible in the thick grass, the bite and claw marks on the kudu indicated that it had, in fact, been killed by a lion.

Gunter was concerned about the amount of meat that had been taken off the kill. The kudu had been reduced almost to a skeleton—something Gunter could not imagine that a single lion could accomplish in only one night. An immediate search of the area turned up no tracks. It was difficult to know whether the lion (or lions, if Gunter was correct in his assumption that a single lion could not have eaten that much of the kill in one night) would remain near the kudu with so little meat remaining.

After checking the kill, Gunter and the others went back up to the lodge, sat on the veranda, and had tea with the landowner and his family as they planned how to kill the lion. This hunt was particularly dangerous because they had no way of knowing the lion's or lions' condition(s), age(s), or attitude(s). That, along with the fact that the lion had shown little fear of man and was possibly responsible for at least one human death, meant that the situation had to be handled with the greatest care. With any luck, Gunter and Jacek would be able to sort out the cat on the open ground near the lion pens and would not have to follow the cat into heavy thorn cover. If the men did, indeed, have to go in and dig the lion out of the thorn and heavy grass, the potential for injury would be great.

Gunter, Jacek, and the members of the family who owned the farm sat on the veranda until the sun had fallen behind the distant hills and a chill settled over the dry plains. The songs of the day birds went

Male lions that are ousted from a pride are forced to find a new territory, sometimes placing them in conflict with humans. (Photo courtesy of Jofie Lamprecht)

quiet and were replaced by the trilling calls of owls and the yap-yap-howl of jackals in the rocky foothills of a distant kopje. At last light, everyone on the veranda leaped to their feet as a series of roars and growls emanated from the pen where the lioness was kept. Running to the edge of the veranda, Schwalm was shocked to see three full-grown male lions, all seemingly in perfect health, battling at the edge of the pen where the lioness was kept. In the fading light, the dust that rose around the fighting lions soon swallowed the cats in a haze so thick that the only proof the cats were there was the snarling and growling that echoed over the plains.

The landowner gathered his wife and children from the yard and returned to the house. With the family safely inside, Gunter and Jacek were left on the edge of the veranda watching as the three males rolled and fought across the open space beside the pen. Jacek's blood ran cold as he stood numbly watching the big cats battle on the plains below. Gunter, even after years in the bush, had never seen anything like the battle raging below, and he realized that this "problem lion" would be exceptionally dangerous. The chase had morphed into taking on three large male lions that were already charged up from the fight over the lioness.

After darkness fell over the farm, the sounds of the lions fighting on the plains below the main house continued in the moonlight. Plans were made to set out in the morning after the lions, since it would be suicide to attempt to hunt them in the late evening. Gunter managed to connect the Namibian authorities and notify them that somehow all of the reports that had filtered in seemed to miss the very important fact that they were dealing with three male lions and not just one. If they were, in fact, man-eaters, these lions posed a tremendous threat to everyone in the vicinity. Battling for the lioness would make them even more aggressive, and in their highly agitated state, they would almost certainly charge if approached.

That night the government granted Gunter Schwalm and his client the right to hunt all three lions, which is rare under any circumstances. Considering the enormous risk these lions posed to the surrounding farms, the government saw fit to allocate three problem-lion permits to Gunter based on his merits as a professional hunter and his insistence that the lions posed a serious threat. All that was left was for Gunter and his client to try to get some sleep before setting out after the lions at dawn.

The next morning broke clear and cold, and the shadow of the great Waterberg massif stretched across the acacia and mopane thickets. It was the dead of winter. Gear was loaded into the truck, and Gunter and Jacek, the events of the night before still fresh in their memories, set out after the three lions. They wouldn't have to go far.

The lioness had done a fine job of holding the attention of the males, which remained in the bush not far from the enclosure and less than a half-mile from the lodge. From the relative safety of the hunting car, Gunter, Jacek, and the trackers watched as the lions stood and moved in a swinging, heavy trot across an open patch of grassland near the enclosure. With rifles at the ready and the hunting car in low gear, the group drove down the hill from the lodge and turned toward the open patch of ground where the males had last been seen. Two of the males, upon hearing the noise of the engine, broke away from their companion. They moved directly toward the hunting car with their heads high and their tails curling left and right. One of the males lowered itself, positioning its legs under its body for the charge. Its companion did the same and the hunters found themselves staring into the cold eyes of two big male lions poised to charge.

Gunter stepped down from the car and told his client to get his rifle ready and make sure his shots counted when the time came. Shivering with cold, Jacek fed cartridges into his rifle as the lions watched. Gunter and Jacek moved cautiously forward, rifles at the ready, and stopped when they had a clear view of the two males lying in wait for them in the bush not far ahead.

"Shoot the one closest to us," Gunter said, the words forming white tendrils of steam that rose out of the corner of his mouth in

The trio of male lions. (Photo courtesy of Gunter Schwalm/Omalanga Safaris)

the cold desert air. When Jacek raised his rifle, Gunter covered the other lion with his own gun, watching the male's steely eyes over the express sights.

Jacek steadied his rifle and found the head of the closest male, seemingly as big and round as a barrel, over the sights of his rifle. He caught half of one breath, held it, and pressed the trigger. The shot connected and the lion slumped in the grass as the big male beside it stood with a growl and started to trot diagonally toward a patch of heavy cover. Jacek worked the bolt of his rifle, flinging the smoking, empty cartridge toward Gunter as he fed a fresh round into the chamber of the rifle. Jacek found the second cat over the sights, held just ahead of the lion's shoulder, and pressed the trigger. When he shot, the cat rose up with a furious thrashing of its tail and a blood-curdling snarl. Jacek fed another round into his rifle and was set to pull the trigger again when the lion collapsed from the first shot.

The third lion then broke from cover and ran perpendicular to the men. Gunter yelled for his client to shoot the cat—and hurry. Jacek swung his rifle ahead of the lion, which was cantering across the open plains, and pressed the trigger. The shot struck the cat just behind the ear and dropped it stone-dead.

As the dust settled, Gunter swung his rifle side-to-side, covering each of the lions in turn. None of them moved. Thanks to some excellent shooting by his client, there had been no follow-up needed and no deadly charge at close range in the thick thornbush. Instead, one client had managed to take three good lions in less than a minute, and the threat they posed to local communities died with the echo of the rifle shots that resonated off the gray walls of the great Waterberg Plateau.

The lions were collected and driven back to the farmhouse. The family members looked into the lifeless eyes of the cats that had terrorized their farm the night before. With great relief, the landowner slapped Jacek on the back and thanked Gunter for helping him deal with the lions before tragedy struck.

Later reports confirmed that at least one of the lions was, in fact, a man-eater.

CHAPTER 20

THE CLIMB

Professional hunter: John Wambach
Location: Gamsberg Mountains

Pete Cottrell thought he had prepared himself for his backpack hunt in the Gamsberg Mountains of Namibia, but a quarter-mile into the hike, with the straps of his heavy pack cutting into his shoulders while the hot desert sun blazed down, he questioned himself. Just ahead of him, moving up over the rocks without slowing, was professional hunter John Wambach. Prior to his hunt, Pete had invested a great deal of time getting physically prepared for the challenge of a backpack zebra hunt in the Mount Barry Wilderness at the edge of the Namib Desert, a hundred miles southwest of the capital of Windhoek. But until he began packing in, climbing the smooth, sun-bleached rockslides with his rifle in his hands, Pete had no appreciation for just how challenging a backpack hunt in one of the world's most remote regions could be.

John kept an eye on his client as they picked their way over the loose, tangerine-colored rocks toward the crest of the ridge. It was early in the day, but the heat was already intense. There would be little relief from the sun and the dust until the men reached the spit of sand in the dried-up bed of the Gaub River that was to serve as their camp for the duration of the hunt.

When they crested the ridge, John paused to survey the landscape that stretched out before them. The rocky hills rose and fell into the shadowed canyon of the Gaub. All around, the rocks were the same burnished color, their faces weathered by eons of hot desert winds and shifting sand. In the valleys, the twisted, leafless trunks of fig and quiver trees sprouted from the open spaces between rockslides, their dry branches like desperate, upturned hands reaching up from the parched earth. On the far horizon, beyond the distant, rocky peaks, John could see the soft roll of the Namib dunes.

The two men started picking their way down the opposite slope, trying not to slip on the loose rocks as they edged cautiously down into

The rocky hills of central Namibia make for a challenging hunt where climbing is part of the game. (Photo courtesy of Jofie Lamprecht)

the rocky drainage, a tributary of the Gaub. John, a seasoned hunter and triathlete, turned back to check on Pete, who was straining under the weight of his pack as he moved from one rock to another down through the drainage. As the midday sun beat down on the men, they finally reached their destination—an oblong patch of sand that backed up against a sheer rock face that rose a thousand feet to the ridge above.

Camp was austere but comfortable. John set up the tents in the shade of a fig tree and unloaded the contents of his pack onto the soft, cool sand. Up and down the length of the river, rough holes had been excavated in the riverbed by the hoofs of thirsty zebras. These holes, dug several feet down into the sand, tapped the contents of underground reservoirs and provided much-needed water for the species living in the Gamsberg Mountains. From the river, John looked up at the slanted rock walls and brittle, dry grass that grew in scattered clumps near the crest.

"Which way do you want to go?" John asked his client. Pete had taken his pack off his back and was having a drink of water after the long hike. His face twisted at the idea of more hiking.

When Pete had regained his strength and had refreshed himself with enough water to consider a climb, he stood in the gray sand of the riverbed and looked up at both of the rock faces. There were rockslides in narrow, dry streambeds up and down the river course that served as uneven stairways to the top of the ridge. Pete surveyed both the left and the right slopes and finally decided.

"Right."

With bags full of water and a rifle slung over Pete's shoulder, the two men started picking their way up to the top, avoiding the scattered thornbushes that somehow managed to eke a living from the dry earth. Here and there they found zebra droppings or fresh hoofprints in the loose, sandy soil. The brittle grass was cropped short by the zebra herds, and the men found several patches of sandy soil pressed flat, an indication that the zebras had been rolling in the dust. Without question, the zebras were using the canyon. It was just a matter of finding them.

The two men had to circumvent a large rock to reach the peak. Once there, John turned and nudged his client, pointing across the canyon at a herd of a half-dozen zebras that stood high-headed and alert, watching the men for a moment before turning and galloping over the rocky soil and disappearing down the opposite side. Pete cursed having chosen the right side of the canyon to climb. If he had suggested the left side, the men would have come up beside the herd and might have been offered a shot.

By the time the men made it back to camp, tired and footsore, the sun was already sliding down behind the western horizon. The canyon was cool, and the growing shadows stretched up the walls as the light faded from orange to red and then to purple. There was no lodge to

The edge of the Namib Desert. (Photo courtesy of Jofie Lamprecht)

come back to every night on this hunt, no fine silverware or feather beds. For John and Pete, sleep would come on a bed of soft, cool desert sand. When the sun finally set and the first stars appeared, they were resting comfortably from the day's hike beside a small quiver-wood fire under a canopy of stars that stretched from one canyon wall to the next and enjoying the cool sand and a piece of dried biltong meat.

Rested and fed, the men sat by the fire, talking quietly over the popping and hissing of the flames. They stopped when a sound came from the slope above them. At first it sounded like a loose rock tumbling down one of the slides. The sound persisted, however, and the clattering grew louder. John smiled and whispered to Pete in the firelight.

"Zebras."

Both men were content to sit and listen as a herd of zebras picked their way down the slope in the moonlight and walked across the sandy bed of the Gaub River not far from the camp. John had seen a fresh patch of sand that the zebras had dug through to find water.

The striking patterns on the backs of Hartmann mountain zebras make them one of the most stunning of all African trophies. (Photo courtesy of Benjamin Gettinger)

After some time, the sound of the clattering rocks came again, growing quieter with each passing moment as the herd ascended the rockslide and the clacking of their hoofs on the stones faded into the night sounds of Africa.

Dawn broke gray and still in the depths of the canyon. Despite the austerity of the camp, Pete had a good night's rest, and in the morning he was ready to set out once again in search of a zebra. That meant a long and difficult climb out of the canyon, picking through rockslides under the weight of his pack and trying not to slip or stumble on the loose stones. After a light breakfast, the men were off, climbing to a plateau high above them.

They scanned the surrounding rocky hillsides from their vantage point, studying yellow grass and dusty rockslides that looked so dry and parched that it seemed impossible to imagine that cooling rains had ever touched this rugged and barren landscape. The distant slopes were covered with short-cropped, amber-colored grass that grew out in irregular furrows between the smooth, weathered crests of rocks buried under the surface of the dry earth.

John got his client's attention and pointed across the plateau at a herd of zebras on a distant ridge. Even at that distance, the zebra herd was wary and managed to catch sight of the men as they moved. The zebras turned and took off at a gallop, disappearing behind a rising cloud of dust that vanished over the far horizon.

The men continued, slipping over the rock piles and climbing across sheer stone faces until they were once again on a vantage point high above the dry plains where they could glass for zebras in the valleys below. John spotted a herd over a mile away and elbowed Pete. The zebras were difficult to see, their stripes blending with the dull background at that distance. Through the shimmering waves of heat that rose up off the plains, Pete finally caught sight of them as they moved through open patches in the rocky ground.

The stalk would not be easy or short, but the men set out. John walked in front and picked his way through the rocks as he closed the

Cunning and skittish, zebras require patience and skill to hunt successfully. (Photo courtesy of John Wambach)

gap on the distant zebra herd. Pete stayed close behind him, feeling the weight of the pack and the uneven sloshing of the water jugs that he was carrying. But there was no time to stop and rest; the herd was moving to the north, and the only hope for John and Pete was to circumvent the next small hill and then climb a rocky ridge in the distance. That would put them above the zebra herd for a possible shot.

As the men neared the top of the ridge where they had planned to glass the herd, John stopped his client and crawled up to the crest alone, keeping low to the ground to avoid being seen by the herd. John saw the zebra herd spread out in the rocks below. The mixed group was scattered across the valley. Right below him, just over a hundred yards away, was a big stallion.

John turned and motioned for Pete to climb the ledge quickly. The stallion was feeding below them, unaware of the men directly above. John gave his client the go-ahead to shoot and watched the stallion through his field glasses as Pete fired. John saw the bullet strike dead center on its shoulder. Over the crash of the rifle's report, John heard the clattering of hoofs on the rocky earth and watched as the stallion ran fifty yards before piling up from the shot.

The men celebrated as they walked down to the stallion. Their packs, once oppressively heavy, were forgotten, and the ankle-breaking rocks seemed of no concern as they made their way to the dead zebra. It was a fine old stallion with a beautifully marked coat.

"Now the real work begins," John said.

It was six miles back to the road over high, rocky crests and down through narrow valleys. John rolled the stallion over and began the work, carefully skinning and then quartering it. The men drank their excess water to make more room in the packs, keeping only enough to get them back to camp. They began quartering the zebra, neatly wrapping each of the quarters and placing them in the packs. Some of the meat they boned out to reduce the staggering weight. Finally, their packs loaded down with hundreds of pounds of meat, they started back toward their camp in the dry Gaub River.

It was slow going over the dry, rocky earth. It was hard to get comfortable under the weight of the packs, and every step, whether climbing a ridge or picking their way down a rockslide, was labored. Pete, sweating under the strain of his pack, was watching John, who also carried the wet zebra hide rolled on his back. Mile after mile they went, slowly mounting each ridge and then descending with slow deliberation until they saw the valley below and their small camp backed up against the rocks in the shade of the quiver tree.

Even with their camp in sight, Pete wasn't sure whether he would make it back to their simple bivouac in the sandy riverbed. He had long since abandoned the practice of picking his way carefully down the ridge. By that time, sweated out under the weight of his trophy and smelling the sweet, musty smell of the meat on his back, Pete pressed on down the hill, no longer avoiding the clumps of *swarthaak* bush that littered the hillside but bowling them over as he made his way down the narrow zebra trails to camp.

Finally, the men reached camp and stopped for a bottle of water and a Coca-Cola that John kept in a cool box. It was late afternoon, and the long shadows were lengthening across the valley. Breezes swept down the canyon walls, carried down the valley on thermals. Pete and John settled back and took a moment to relax, enjoying the untouched wilderness of the Gamsberg Mountains and reliving the best moments of the hunt. They could not wait long, though. There was still work to be done. They shouldered their packs once again and headed for the road.

CHAPTER 21

The Devil in Black and White

Professional hunter: Bijorn le Roux
Location: Etosha Conservancy

There is an age-old debate about which of Africa's big-game animals is the most dangerous. The question itself is largely relative and depends a great deal upon circumstances and conditions; most professional hunters can argue back and forth for hours about the merits of one species over another. The result is almost always a draw.

When asked about the most tenacious animal, however, most PHs are in agreement. Pound for pound, this beast is capable of doing more damage and taking more abuse than perhaps any other African animal. It is not the buffalo or any of Africa's big cats. In fact, it is not a classic game species at all. It is the honey badger, or ratel, a relative of the North American badger and a member of the Mustelidae family, which includes skunks and weasels. Even the *Guinness Book of World Records* recognized the honey badger as the world's most fearless animal.

At first glance, the honey badger appears ambling and almost awkward. Like most members of Mustelidae, honey badgers are built low to the ground and their long bodies are supported by thick legs with large paws equipped with long nails that allow them to rip apart logs, honeycombs, and even termite mounds. Insects and snakes make up the bulk of the badger's diet, but as the name implies, they are also well known for following African honey guide birds to beehives and feeding on the combs amid swarms of furious bees.

The honey badger's reputation for tenacity is well earned. They will attempt to drive larger predators, including leopards and hyenas, from their kills, and often their furious rages are effective, persuading the larger carnivores to abandon their kills rather than risk a fight. Honey badgers disregard the stings of scorpions and bees and have even been known to survive bites from venomous snakes. *National Geographic* filmmakers captured footage of a young male honey badger being bitten

Bijorn le Roux, photographer Veronica Gettinger, and the author on safari in the Etosha Conservancy. (Photo courtesy of Benjamin Gettinger)

by a deadly puff adder, falling comatose and apparently dead beside its kill, then rising hours later to finish its meal!

Honey badgers are ever-present on most Namibian safaris and it is rare not to find badger tracks in hunting camp. They are also a major problem for leopard hunters because honey badgers will take over any bait they find and the cat rarely reappears once a badger has taken up residence at the bait. In areas where honey badgers are thick, this can mean one lost opportunity after another.

PH Bijorn le Roux of Mashete Safaris was having a difficult time hanging leopard baits because each time he would hang one, the badgers would quickly claim it as their own. Mashete's base of operations is the vast Etosha Conservancy, a million-acre communal conservancy that stretches from the central highlands north to the border of Etosha National Park through the Kunene region, a land dominated by rolling, rocky hills and vast, flat plains of tall grass interrupted here and there by squatty acacias. In the northern portion of the conservancy, near the southern border of Etosha Park, the landscape shifts and the grassy plains become more densely wooded. From north to south, the whole of the Etosha Conservancy is a prime area for leopards, and each year many big cats are taken in the area. The conservancy is also home to a healthy population of honey badgers.

In the stale midday heat Bijorn stood at the base of the bait tree and examined the zebra carcass that was being swarmed by bottle flies. There had been a nice tom leopard visiting the bait at one time, but the comma-shaped pug marks and black-and-white hair caught in the bark of the tree told him that a honey badger had visited the bait site and caused the leopard to move off in search of another meal. Bijorn turned and relayed the news of the honey badger's raid to his client, who was visibly disappointed by the news that the cat would likely not return.

Rifle on rack for early morning hunt in the Etosha Conservancy. (Photo courtesy of Benjamin Gettinger)

The story was all too familiar, as Bijorn had lost other baits to badgers in the same area over the course of the previous weeks.

A new bait site was established. Another zebra flank was wired to the lowest limbs of a scraggly tree, and it wasn't long before a roving leopard caught wind of the offering and began feeding on the bait. The morning after hanging the bait, the hunters could tell that a big tom had eaten its fill and spent considerable time in the area. The cat was feeding well, shearing off great chunks of the graying flesh and eating the zebra flank down to the chipped and cracked remains of the leg bone. *Perhaps,* Bijorn thought, *my run of bad luck has finally ended.*

When the cat was feeding regularly, Bijorn and his men constructed a blind that would give them a good view of the limb in the late hours of evening, which was when the cat would be most likely to feed. The hunting party settled into the blind at midday. Bijorn adjusted his client's rifle on a makeshift rest of acacia limbs. After checking the field of view through the scope and making various adjustments to the makeshift rest, Bijorn had everything set so the cross hairs rested just above the limb where the leopard would most likely be standing when it came to feed. Bijorn's men left the blind, and hunter and client settled in for the hours they would spend waiting for the cat to return to the pilfered kill. With any luck, the leopard would reappear before dark.

The high anticipation that fills a leopard blind for the first hour of the wait had faded into monotonous, sleepy frustration. Guinea fowls cackled and moved in a scattered cluster at the base of the tree, emitting their obnoxious call, *urrr-tur-tur-tur,* as they pecked at the dry, gray soil and chased one another through the tufts of long grass. Daylight was fading to darkness, and after the troop of guineas left and the dust raised by their pecking and scratching finally settled, long shadows stretched across the plain. The coming of the night was still and silent. Not long after the sun disappeared below the distant hilltops, the landscape turned deep red. The light dropped and shadows overtook the plains as the western horizon became a

Sunset found the hunters waiting for the arrival of the leopard; however, another African predator decided to feed upon the bait. (Photo courtesy of Jacques Strauss)

haze of red and orange. It was the hour of the leopard, the time when any glance up toward the limb might find the hunters eye-to-eye with Africa's stealthiest hunter.

The plains were silent. Not even the go-away birds called, and the guineas, long departed, had roosted in some far-off place. The evening turned a deep shade of purple. In a few moments it would be too dark to hunt, and the men would have to call an end to their patrol. Just before the last shooting light was swallowed by darkness, Bijorn heard a faint but unmistakable sound: the dry rasp of claws against bark. He leaned forward and told his client to be ready—there was something in the tree. The sound came again, louder and unmistakable in the stillness. The animal pulled itself farther into the tree, gaining purchase with its claws and hauling itself into the branches.

Bijorn watched the bait through his binocular. The flies that covered the bait during midday had abandoned the kill. No more swarms circled like a macabre halo over the torn and half-eaten leg. Bijorn looked around the bait to see if he could see the cat anywhere on the ground. The rasping of claws against bark could be heard once more, and Bijorn was convinced that the cat was in the tree. He turned to his client.

"Wait," Bijorn whispered. "Be ready." He saw his client settle down against the wooden stock as he continued to scan the tree.

The rifle erupted and the stillness of the evening was broken by the resounding muzzle blast and a flash of flame that burst into the darkness like a sudden pulse of lightning. Bijorn jumped back and cursed, lowering his binocular and trying to figure out if his client had seen the cat and taken a shot, or if he had, in a moment of great excitement, touched the trigger accidentally. Just as he turned to ask his client why on earth he had decided to shoot, Bijorn heard the unmistakable meaty thump of an animal falling from the tree. Even through the remnant of muzzle flash that still burned in front of his eyes, Bijorn could see a plume of dust rising from the foot of the tree.

"What did you do?" Bijorn asked.

"I shot him! I shot the leopard! Didn't you see him there?" His client was wide-eyed with excitement.

The client was very excited to see his prize, but Bijorn had his doubts and was more than a little nervous about walking up on a wounded leopard that he had not yet seen. They waited, listening for any additional sounds from the base of the tree. There were none. There had been only the single, heavy *whack* of the animal hitting the ground amid the echo of the fading rifle shot.

Bijorn turned on his flashlight and swung it in a wide arc as he approached the tree, ready to shoot at the first sign of movement. As he circled the bait tree he saw a black body lying outstretched in the sand. He turned to his client, who stood some distance back. Bijorn turned the light toward him and saw the look of intense satisfaction on his client's face.

Jeremiah, Mashete's head tracker, is barely visible at the top of this tree as he scouts for game in the surrounding plains. (Photo courtesy of Benjamin Gettinger)

"You shot a honey badger."

To the client's credit, it had been one heck of a shot, sending the bullet through the bait and catching the offending badger between the front legs. It had been a swift, precise kill. The honey badger lay sprawled in the dust at the base of the tree, looking mean even in death and still clinging furiously to the last flesh it would ever eat.

Bijorn asked his client what on earth had prompted him to shoot the honey badger. His client told him very calmly that he had seen a furry paw come over the top of the bait and that he had centered the cross hairs on the center of the zebra leg and pressed the trigger. Bijorn did not know what to say as they stood in awkward silence looking down at the honey badger.

Night had fallen, and the first stars appeared in the blue sky toward the east. Through the darkness, Bijorn heard the sound of the hunting car's motor as his men headed back to the blind, certainly filled with great excitement about hearing the shot. They would anticipate finding a big tom leopard stretched out under the tree. Bijorn tried to piece together the words to explain to them what had really happened.

The client, though, did not seem terribly upset. Leopard or none, he would go home with a fine honey badger cape and a one-of-a-kind story of mistaken identity.

CHAPTER 22

The Nomads of the Kalahari

Professional hunter: Joof Lamprecht
Location: Kalahari

Dawn broke over the cold Kalahari Desert. Long, purple shadows stretched over the red sand and the pale grass appeared the color of sun-bleached bone in the rising light of morning. Professional hunter Joof Lamprecht of Hunters Namibia Safaris and his client, Hal, sat still and silent in their leopard blind, watching the empty branch with the bait wired to it. Leopard hunting is always a test of patience and will, and so far the big tom that was hitting the bait simply refused to show itself during daylight hours.

The rising sun chased away the chill of night, and the desert came alive through the narrow window of the blind. A troop of helmeted guinea fowls dawdled under the bait tree, scratching and stirring the white sand and chasing each other through the morning light. Shy doves landed in the red sand between the tufts of grass and moved in small circles, bobbing their heads and picking through the dead grass for loose seeds. A lilac-breasted roller sat high in the thorny crown of the green acacia and preened its shimmering emerald and purple feathers. When it had finished, the bird puffed all of its feathers out and shook its whole body, warmed and ready for the day. The leopard, however, did not appear.

When daylight began streaming through the opening in the blind, Joof tapped his client on the shoulder and they both stood, stretching as they stepped out of the narrow confines of the blind. It had been a long morning, and it felt good to move through the warm morning light. Still, mere warmth was small consolation after spending long hours in the blind, staring at the tattered, fly-blown bait with no sign of the leopard.

The two men started back toward the truck, enjoying the warmth on their muscles as they made their way back up toward the road. Overhead, the morning sky was cloudless blue and the thin, green

Cheetahs roam over vast areas and are very difficult to find. They do not hold at bait like leopards, and many cheetahs are taken incidentally when hunters come across them while pursuing other game. **(Photo courtesy of Jofie Lamprecht)**

leaves of the camelthorn trees shuddered in the light breeze. With luck, the wind would stay low. The men had already had enough problems on the hunt for the big tom leopard, and a steady wind would only be another setback. Getting the leopard to the bait site during daylight hours had required many hours of preparation. They had located a good site, constructed a blind that afforded a good view yet remained hidden, shot and hung baits, and put in many hours of waiting in the blind. Now all that Joof and his client required was a bit of good luck.

When they reached the red, sandy two-track, Joof thought their luck had changed. There were large pug marks pressed deep into the sand. But these were not the tracks of the leopard. Instead, these were cheetah prints. Joof stooped over the prints and examined them. The spoor was very fresh; the edges of the prints were still sharp and clean, which meant that the cheetahs had passed by in the last few hours while Joof and Hal sat in the blind only a few hundred yards away.

Cheetahs are one of the most difficult prizes to obtain in Namibia. Unlike lions and leopards, which can be baited, cheetahs prefer fresh meat and generally will not visit bait sites. In addition, cheetahs wander over very large home ranges, following game or patrolling the invisible boundaries of their territories across miles of thorn thickets and open plains. One of the few successful methods for intercepting cheetahs is to catch them visiting a "play tree," a communal marking post that passing cheetahs use to announce their presence to others in an effort to defend or secure territory or find a mate. But catching a male cheetah at a play tree requires tremendous luck and a great deal of time. Most cheetahs in Namibia are taken by chance, and by the looks of the fresh pugs pressed deep in the soft red sand, it seemed that Hal's luck had taken a turn for the better. Because of U.S. Fish & Wildlife Service restrictions, Hal would not be allowed to take the cheetah's skin back to the United States, but Hal understood this and still agreed to the hunt.

Joof consulted his tracker, a bush veteran named Johnny "Zeiss Eyes." Johnny immediately set out on the track, weaving back and forth slowly across the two-track as he studied the overlapping prints.

Although they have been eradicated in other parts of Africa, cheetah populations in Namibia remain strong. Even so, getting a cat is a difficult proposition. (Photo courtesy of Benjamin and Veronica Gettinger/Crisp Photography)

Johnny's verdict matched Joof's: A big male cheetah was following a female in estrous.

The men set out in single file, Johnny leading the group while Joof and Hal followed closely behind him. The cheetah pair continued down the road. The male seemed to give the female a wide berth, walking off to the side and only occasionally following directly in the female's tracks.

Joof did not rush. Having made his living hunting wild game in Namibia for three decades, Joof had learned the traits of all the game, including cheetahs. Cheetahs, he knew, relied heavily on their eyesight and preferred to lie on high points like rocks, low-hanging branches, and termite mounds in order to see anything that approached them. If the wandering Kalahari cheetahs found such a place and caught sight

Rainstorm in the Kalahari. **(Photo courtesy of Jacques Strauss)**

of the men approaching, the stalk would immediately be blown and the cats would be out of range in minutes.

The cheetah pair continued down the road, moving without haste through the waist-high yellow grass. By late morning, the sun was high and the coolness of early morning was swallowed in the heat and haze. The tracks, which had been plainly visible in the morning light, were now washed-out by the intense midday sun. The men had slowed, partly in an effort not to be seen, but also because the long hours of sitting in the blind combined with miles of stooping and slipping through the grass were taking a toll.

Joof paused and stood looking out over the plains. Ahead of them, rising from the dry savanna, stood a rock kopje. High, smooth walls of

stone towered over the surrounding grassy veld. The base of the rock pile was circled by leafy camelthorn trees that grew at obtuse angles from the sand, their crooked trunks supporting wide green canopies where the bulging nests of sociable weaverbirds hung like great, straw-colored umbrellas from the topmost branches. Joof knew that the cheetah pair was likely looking for a place to rest in the heat of midday, and the low, cool rocks in the shade at the base of the kopje would be just the place for them to spend the long afternoon hours. The men slowed their approach even more, moving only a few feet at a time as they scanned the low rocks for a twitching ear or lashing tail. Step-by-step the men approached, moving in a huddled group as they drew closer to the rocks. Joof could not escape the feeling that the cats were there.

A hundred yards from the kopje, Johnny stopped, fixing his gaze on a camelthorn tree at the base of the kopje. There, stretched out full-length on one of the low-hanging branches of the tree, was the male cheetah. Joof raised his glasses to double-check that this was indeed the cat they were after. The thick neck, rounded ears, and square head verified what Johnny had said, and Joof told Hal that if he wanted a cheetah he had better take careful aim and fire quickly. He knew that the moment the male caught sight of them, it would slip down from the branch and disappear into the yellow grass like a snake into its hole.

Hal steadied his rifle on the shooting sticks and found the cat's chest in the cross hairs of the scope. When Hal pressed the trigger, the 7mm Remington Magnum recoiled with a flash and a roar. Joof watched as the cat slumped and slid down into the tall grass at the base of the tree. The female rose up and ran off, vanishing into the tall grass without a sound.

They found the male under the limb where it had been lying. The shot had killed it instantly, and the cat lay stretched out at full length under the tree. Joof, Hal, and Johnny shared congratulatory words as they stood in awe of the great cat, its lithe body longer than any of the men, its deep chest and long legs built for ultimate speed. Although the leopard hunt had been long and frustrating, Hal's luck had changed. He had procured one of Africa's rarest and most elusive trophies.

CHAPTER 23

The Tomb

Professional hunter: Maré van der Merwe
Location: Khomas Hochland

Cats play a major role in African culture and theology. In Egypt, they served as symbols of cleverness and wisdom, and many ancient Egyptian gods and kings were traditionally personified in feline form. King Tut's tomb provided evidence that he was buried with his cats so that they might accompany him into the afterlife as a measure of protection and good fortune. Native peoples across the continent revered and respected felines of various species, from the diminutive African wildcat to the regal lion.

No cat on the African continent, however, has proven more adaptable and cunning than the leopard. It is at once elusive and ferocious, capable of slipping silently within reach of prey or forcing home a point-blank charge when wounded and pursued. Its coat was highly valued by fur traders in Europe, Asia, and the Americas. Despite intense hunting pressure and a tremendous demand for their pelts, leopard populations have remained stable across much of their original range, which covers most of the African continent from the Cape of Good Hope to Egypt and along the fringes of the Sahara. This serves as testimony to the leopard's ability to vanish into thick cover and exist in good numbers even when surrounded by those who pursue it, often leaving nothing more than pug marks in the sand. While lion and cheetah numbers have declined dramatically, the leopard remains the elusive observer that lurks in the shadows.

Leopard hunting is one of the most specialized of all African pursuits. When setting out to take a leopard, it is essential to have a professional hunter who has experience in hunting cats. One such hunter is Maré van der Merwe of African Twilight Safaris, a firm based in the famed Khomas Hochland Conservancy in the high, rocky hills of central Namibia.

Setting out at dawn to hunt. (Photo courtesy of Jacques Strauss)

The conservancy is an example of the benefits of cooperation between Namibian landowners and hunting outfitters. The Khomas Hochland is a half-million-acre conglomeration of farms and hunting ranches that is home to a tremendous variety of plains-game species. The dry hills and sandstone canyons meet thick acacia veld—the perfect landscape to support endemic species such as kudus, oryxes, and Hartmann mountain zebras as well as a variety of introduced species such as black wildebeests and blesboks. This abundance of prey also means that most of the sandy two-track roads within the conservancy are littered with the spoor of big leopards.

Leopard hunting is always strenuous. Maré knew this, and when his American client, Wendell Harsanyi, indicated that taking a big leopard was the top priority for his upcoming safari, Maré set out to find him just the cat he was looking for. The short thornbush and deep canyons of the Khomas Hochland make it ideal leopard habitat, but the scant vegetation and stubby trees offered very few possible locations for baits or blinds. The best course of action, as Maré saw it, was to set baits to draw leopards to the area, find fresh spoor, and then use hounds to locate and bay the cat in the surrounding hills. (Hunting leopards with hounds was discontinued shortly after this hunt took place and is no longer practiced in Namibia.)

All leopard hunts are high-stakes affairs where the cat must be located and shot during a relatively short period of ten to fifteen days. With so much pressure on the PH, it is essential to find a capable houndsman who understands both dogs and cats. Maré enlisted the aid of South Africa's Glenn Nel and his famed "Bongolo" hounds, Nel's nickname for his pack of dogs.

Prior to the outlawing of hound hunting, Nel's outstanding pack of hounds led hunters to many of Namibia's largest record-book cats. But hunting in the arid canyons of the Khomas Hochland with hounds was a difficult task that required finding extremely fresh spoor and following it with seasoned dogs. These dogs would have to be capable of sorting the minimal scent out of the dry sand and rocks. Conditions in the Khomas Hochland are among the most difficult in Namibia for hounds, and the only hope was to draw the cat to bait in order to set the dogs on a very fresh track. Once the cat was feeding well, the hounds would be turned loose at first light, just after the tom had left the bait and gone into the rocks to wait out the heat of the day.

On the fifth day of the hunt, a springbok bait that the hunters had secured in a dry riverbed went missing. Maré led his client down to where they had left the bait the day before. The cat's movements from the previous night were clearly documented in the dry sand of the riverbed: The big, round pug marks straddled the depression that showed where the cat had dragged the springbok down the riverbed, stopping occasionally to adjust its grip until it had carried the bait more than a quarter mile and stopped to begin feeding. Maré, Harsanyi, and the trackers found the kill where the leopard had left it in a clump of thorn at the edge of the dry riverbed—the dead springbok's backside and paunch partially eaten. Afterward, the leopard had left the kill, sauntered to the base of the hill, and then climbed up into the rocks to spend the hot midday hours.

It was first light when the hunters came upon the remains of the springbok. The spoor appeared very fresh, and Glenn and Maré agreed that the big tom had been feeding very shortly before the men arrived.

Glenn pulled his two best hounds from the truck—a matched pair of lanky foxhound/blue-tick crosses named Sharky and Rose. The two dogs leaped down on top of the track and began slowly working back and forth, wagging their long tails and shuffling the dirt and sand with their noses as they breathed in the scent of the leopard. The brace of hounds started off into the mountains, working the track with slow deliberation up the hillsides and into the heavy cover where the old tom spent the hot afternoons. Soon the trail grew fresher and the hounds went into full cry, their howls echoing down the sandstone walls as they worked up and over the top of the ridge. Not far ahead of them, the tom worked its way down the opposite side of the canyon, slipping without a sound down the featureless rock face and up the next sheer slope. Soon the voices of the hounds faded and the men were left in the silence of the canyon where they had turned the dogs loose.

Glenn worked his way up the mountain in pursuit of the hounds as Maré and Harsanyi set out in the truck in an effort to catch the cat when it made its stand. The sun was well up two hours later, but the hounds continued on the trail, working along the crest of a second

A trail camera catches a big leopard on bait. (Photo courtesy of Jaco van der Merwe)

rocky ridge before pushing the tom down into the shadowy base of the opposite riverbed. It was there that the tom stopped to face the dogs. Three hours after the race had started, Maré and Wendell caught up to the hounds and the bayed tom. It had made its final stand in a rock pile at the bottom of the canyon where it remained hidden from the men in a dark cave among the boulders. The only evidence that the big cat was in the tomblike hole was the furious baying of the hounds at the edge of the lair, and the occasional roar that echoed out of the dark heart of the cave.

Neither man nor dog stood a chance against the tom while it remained in its bivouac among the rocks, which also acted as an amphitheater for its guttural snarls and roars. Despite the bawling hounds that pressed against the entrance to the cave—only to be driven back with a swipe of a paw—the cat remained safe within its stone fortress. It could remain there indefinitely until its pursuers gave up and went away.

Maré and Glenn decided that if Harsanyi was ever to have his chance at the old tom, the cat would have to be forced out of the rocks. To prompt the leopard out of the cave, Glenn released three more hounds, which quickly found their way to the rock pile and joined Sharky and Rose at the mouth of the cave. Emboldened by their increase in forces, the dogs worked forward into the dark rim of the cave and the snarls and roars from inside grew louder and more furious until the cat finally turned and slipped out through another hole in the rocks.

The chase spilled down the riverbed, the cat roaring and running in front, tail lashing and ears pinned, as the dogs followed in full voice. Maré ordered Harsanyi to shoot as the cat made for the next outcropping. Harsanyi shouldered his .300 magnum and fired as the cat passed him just over a hundred yards away. Miraculously, the shot connected, though its effects were not known since the cat continued up into the rocks with the pack roaring behind.

The dogs continued to bay among the huge boulders, but the men had no idea whether or not the leopard was dead. Based on the shot

Trophy leopard taken on the hunt with Maré van der Merwe of African Twilight Safaris. (Photo courtesy of Maré van der Merwe)

and the behavior of his Bongolo pack, Glenn believed that the odds were in the hunters' favor and that the cat was dead among the rocks above. He went as far as to give odds, saying there was an 80 percent chance the leopard was dead.

It was the other 20 percent that Maré worried about. A bayed, wounded leopard was deadly. Climbing into the rocks after a wounded cat amounted to suicide, and Maré wasn't going to risk an encounter with the cat while it was still mobile. The men waited an hour. When the time had passed without any indication that the leopard was fighting the dogs or making its escape, Maré moved in among the orange boulders.

They found the old cat lying dead among the rocks. Harsanyi's shot had been excellent—he had connected with the tom while it was in full flight and at more than one hundred yards away. The cat was old and heavy with numerous scars on its beautiful anthracite-and-pale-yellow coat. As the sun set over the Khomas Hochland, the men loaded the old cat onto their shoulders and took it down from its rocky tomb and back to camp.

CHAPTER 24

Lucky 72

Professional hunter: Allan Cilliers
Location: Caprivi

Professional hunter Allan Cilliers did not believe in cutting corners, particularly when it came to searching for big ivory. Allan's hunting concession in Bwabwata National Park near the Kwando River consistently produced some of the best elephants in Namibia, and the bulls in that region were among the largest of any on the continent. They weighed close to six tons and sported the classic Caprivi tusks, which are extremely thick and heavy, but shorter than ivory from eastern elephants. Although he could have simplified hunting in his concession by cutting a series of roads throughout the mopane forests and establishing water points that would draw in and hold game animals such as elephants, buffaloes, and sables, Cilliers elected instead to hunt elephants on foot by tracking. Hunters planning to hire Allan had better count on paying for their ivory with shoe leather.

When Spanish hunter Paco Ross contacted Cilliers about an elephant hunt in the Kwando region, Cilliers was happy to oblige, especially considering the fact that Ross had chosen Cilliers based on the testimony of the great Spanish elephant hunter Tony Sanchez-Ariño. Hunting on foot for a big elephant in the Terminalia forests of the Kwando is never easy, so Cilliers was taken aback when his client told him that he was eighty-two years old. Further, Ross wanted to bring along his son, Gerrman, who also wanted to bag an elephant. The hunters wanted to try to take both elephants in a ten-day hunt.

Cilliers knew it wouldn't be easy to take a single big bull in ten days, let alone two. But his hunters seemed dedicated and focused on the mission. Allan explained how hard hunting on the Kwando would be, but his clients insisted they could handle the heat and the miles. The dates were set, and Paco and Gerrman arrived in Windhoek determined to accomplish something that would require dedication, long hours, dusty miles, and a tremendous amount of luck.

Namibia is home to some of the biggest elephants in Africa; however, getting close to a good bull often requires a great deal of hard walking. **(Photo courtesy of Benjamin and Veronica Gettinger)**

Herd of elephants drinking in the Caprivi Strip, northern Namibia. (Photo courtesy of Allan Cilliers)

Paco Ross may have been an octogenarian, but he certainly had plenty of experience hunting elephants. Having already shot seventy-one bulls in his lifetime, Ross was among the handful of international hunters in the modern era who had taken dozens of elephants—something that was commonplace during the days of the ivory trade but is exceedingly rare today. Cilliers worried about Ross's ability to walk long miles in the heat of Caprivi, but his client was aware of the conditions of the hunt and still wanted to try his luck.

Great herds of elephants congregate every year in the reedbeds and acacia forests along the edges of the Kwando during the dry

season. Although these elephants can gather in herds in excess of three hundred animals, Cilliers knew that the odds of finding a good bull in open cover along the river's edge during daylight hours was slim. In fact, in the entire time he had operated in the concession, the best bull Cilliers had ever encountered along the river sported just forty pounds of ivory.

Therefore, Cilliers and his men traveled inland, away from the Kwando River, into the dry heart of the concession. Allan brought his clients to his camp near Delta Pan, a secluded water hole twenty-five miles inland from the Kwando River.

Almost immediately, Cilliers and his clients found the spoor of a group of bulls. The tracks were large and fresh, which was a good sign, although the size of a bull's feet do not necessarily correlate to tusk size or quality. When two of the bulls split off from the group of eleven, Cilliers decided that the best chance of finding good ivory was to follow the pair that had slipped away from the others. During his years as a PH, Cilliers had rarely found good ivory in large bachelor herds. More often, he found the biggest bulls living in smaller groups in deeper cover and far from human settlements. In addition, larger bachelor groups tended to travel faster than groups of two or three bulls, and since they were already a good distance from the car and the midday temperature was quickly increasing, Cilliers decided to set out on the trail of the brace of bulls that had separated from the others.

The men set out on the dusty trail in single file with Allan and his tracker at the front. As the sun rose higher and the heat of midday became more intense, the group had to stop frequently to allow Paco to rest. Tracking was slow in the heavy mix of Terminalia and Burkea. As the sun crested and started descending toward the western horizon, one of Cilliers's trackers stopped the group with the upturned palm of his hand. There was a faint rumbling and a peeling sound from the thicket of thorn just ahead. The sounds were followed by a sudden, sharp crack as a wrist-thick limb was wrenched from a fallen tree.

Cilliers turned to look at his clients. They had caught up to the bulls.

In order to get a look at the ivory, Cilliers and Gerrman, who was to have the first shot at a good bull, would have to slip farther into the Terminalia and hope that neither of the bulls would hear them or catch their scent on the fickle breeze. If the men were detected at such close range in heavy cover, the outcome would likely be a point-blank charge.

Cilliers moved with his client alongside him until the first great, mud-colored ear appeared through the limbs ahead of them. Bit by bit, the elephant appeared as a patchwork of earthy gray hide behind the veil of thorns and branches. In the shadow of the forest,

Cilliers saw that one of the bulls, the closer one, had thick, sap-stained tusks that hung far down from its lip. He gave the thumbs up and motioned for his client to follow as they jockeyed through the thorns for a clear shot.

When they were within thirty yards of the elephants, Cilliers put his hand out to stop Gerrman. Client and hunter had already discussed shot placement under various circumstances, and from their vantage point with the elephant's broad shoulder looming above them, Cilliers signaled that his client should take the high-percentage heart/lung shot. Gerrman raised his .500 Nitro Express double rifle, found the front leg and shoulder of the bull over the shallow-V sight, and held the irons just above the folded flap of skin behind the front leg. When the sight picture looked good, Gerrman pressed the front trigger. The .500 rose up with a roar and Gerrman was rocked back with the recoil,

This was an eighty-three-pound bull taken with PH Allan Cilliers in the Caprivi. (Photo courtesy of Allan Cilliers)

but he found the second trigger almost immediately and sent another 570-grain slug into the broad gray shoulder of the bull, striking the lungs. Long seconds passed as the bull turned in three rapid circles, steadied itself, and then charged to the right of the men, the echoing of the rifle shots lost in the furious trumpeting and snapping of saplings and dead limbs. The bull Gerrman had shot faltered and crashed down into the Terminalia thirty yards from the men.

The forest fell silent as they approached the elephant. After an insurance shot raised a cloud of dust from the bull's back, the handshakes and backslapping commenced. The other bull was gone, and the men circled the dead bull, which was still veiled by a thin cloud of dust that had risen when it fell. They celebrated with a shot of lukewarm water as the bull was butchered. The bloody tusks, which weighed 69 and 72 pounds, were cut from their sockets and wrapped for transport back to the main camp. It was an excellent bull and would have been the highlight of most any safari; however, their excitement was tempered since the grand old bull that Gerrman had taken was only one of the two that the Rosses had come to Bwabwata for.

The following day, Gerrman got his chance to connect with a gnarly old Caprivi buffalo. Afterward, Paco and Allan set out to search the Delta Pan area for another elephant bull that would match Gerrman's. This time, the elephant hunting was not so easy. Cilliers and the others cut tracks and followed them each day, but none of the bulls they found carried more than sixty pounds of ivory. Paco was willing to take any one of the large fifty-pounders, but Cilliers convinced his client that there would be a chance at a bigger, heavier bull if he had patience and was able to walk the many miles of narrow, thorny trails required to look over a few more bulls. During the week that followed, however, Cilliers himself began to question whether or not he could find one of the big sixty-pound-plus bulls he knew were around.

By the ninth day of the hunt, Cilliers had redirected his efforts to another section of the concession, fifty miles west of the Delta Pan hunting area where Gerrman had killed his bull. It wasn't very long after arriving at his new camp, which was less than three miles from the border of Angola, that Cilliers found the spoor of a large herd of bulls crossing a two-track road. It took time, but Cilliers's trackers eventually determined that there were thirteen bulls. Under normal circumstances, Cilliers would have continued on since he knew that big, shootable bulls rarely traveled with large herds. But the tracks were extremely fresh and time was limited. Cilliers decided to follow the tracks to take a look at the bulls instead of taking a risk and continuing on in search of other bulls. Paco had proven himself to be a thoroughly capable elephant hunter despite his age, and he had impressed Cilliers greatly a few days before when they had tracked six bulls for almost ten miles.

At first, Cilliers worried that following the tracks of the big herd might prove to be a waste of what little time remained on the safari since the elephants were moving quickly toward the edge of the concession. But after an hour and a half of tracking, the men finally caught up with the thirteen bulls and found the herd loafing in a scattered group at the edge of cover. Cilliers and his client moved up to the edge of a small clearing and systematically checked the bulls through field glasses, giving each piece of ivory a thorough examination while the elephants fed along the border of the forest and the grassy plains. Finally, Cilliers lowered his glasses. Nothing. There was not a bull over fifty-five pounds in the herd. Just as Cilliers had expected, the large herd was made up of mostly small, immature bulls. He watched them slowly work their way along the forest's edge, fanning their ears in the heat of late afternoon.

Fifty yards to their right, a fourteenth bull appeared. It was moving slowly among the trees and Terminalia. This last bull was much larger than any other elephant in the herd, and Cilliers turned and told his client that this was the one they wanted and to get ready. They would only have to cover a few yards before they would have a clean shot at the bull's shoulder.

Without warning, the wind changed direction and alerted the herd to the presence of the men. They raised the alarm and ran off in different directions in the bush, their heads and tails high, and the green savanna seemed to swallow all of the bulls at once. Only one of them, the largest, turned in the opposite direction. Cilliers motioned for his client to follow and together they ran into the green Terminalia thicket on the heels of the big bull.

The big tusker was quietly feeding almost a half-mile away from its original location when Cilliers and his men caught up to it. It was impossible to stalk silently in the heavy cover and the wind had already betrayed them once, so Cilliers and Paco slipped from one broad patch of Terminalia to the next until they were within thirty-five yards of the bull. Paco lifted his .416 Rigby rifle and let it settle on the shooting sticks, trying to sort out the bull's shoulder amid the mosaic of elephant gray and spring green.

When the rifle erupted and snapped back with recoil, the whole thicket seemed to shudder with the muzzle blast. Cilliers saw a small, white puff of dust erupt from the elephant's side. The bull turned and started for the forest again but made it only seventy yards before succumbing to Paco's perfect heart shot. The bull collapsed, as elephants often do, on the side where it had been shot.

Soon Cilliers's men began the hard work of butchering the elephant, their second of the week. When the tusks were pulled, they tipped the scales at 64 and 66 pounds, a fantastic old Caprivi bull. Paco was well pleased with his seventy-second elephant. In fact, a few years later, he booked with Allan Cilliers once again and returned to the Terminalia thickets of the Kwando concession in Namibia to collect his eightieth elephant. For Paco, who had hunted elephants all across the African continent, the lure of returning to Caprivi was simply too much to resist.

CHAPTER 25

The Roaring

Professional hunter: Dirk de Bod
Location: Onguma Game Reserve

The sun was setting through the limbs of distant acacias, their branches forming a spider's web of shadows over the dry sand in front of the leopard blind inside which Dirk de Bod and his client Donna Boddington sat in silence watching the bait tree. In the fading light, the tallow-colored bait appeared marbled and glossy against the dull gray bark of the limb where the meat was lashed with heavy wires. All around the blind, the chorus of the African evening was going full tilt. Doves cooed in the orange light, and far off in the flat-topped trees, a go-away bird gave a nasal call that faded out over the plains. The dusty heat of day was giving way to the chill of evening as the sky turned from blue to lavender. Time was running out.

Dirk de Bod. (Photo courtesy of Dirk de Bod Safaris)

Dirk and Craig had a rare opportunity to hunt a lion on a problem-animal permit, a license issued by the Ministry of Environment and Tourism. (Photo courtesy of Karl Stumpfe)

Two days before, Donna, Craig, and Brittany Boddington had arrived at Windhoek for a safari with Dirk at his North East Camp, a collection of luxury tents and a main lodge built on the rolling, tall-grass savanna at the western edge of the Kalahari Plateau. Dirk had been setting baits prior to the arrival of his hunters, but he had no luck bringing in a big tom. There was certainly a good deal of leopard activity, but the only cats that fed on the baits were females and half-grown cubs. Dirk confessed to Craig by the light of a smoking fire on the first night in camp that the leopard sign he was seeing did not look promising. Craig assured him that there was still plenty of time. As a seasoned safari veteran, Craig understood that leopard hunting was a game of patience.

Early the next morning, Dirk and the Boddingtons climbed into the hunting truck and set out to check the baits once more. The result was the same as it had been in the days leading up to the arrival of the Boddingtons: The baits had been hit by leopards, and some had been fed on, but none of the tracks appeared to be those of a big tom.

At noon on the second day of the safari, Dirk and his clients returned to camp without having seen any sign of a male leopard in the area. Word had come down from Danny Bartlett, manager of Onguma Game Reserve, that a big tom had been hitting baits regularly at the reserve, and he asked if Dirk and the Boddingtons would be interested in coming up for a hunt. With any luck, the cat would continue feeding and Donna would have her chance at a big cat in the next few days. The decision was made to move operations to Onguma that afternoon and to hunt from a blind overlooking where the big male had been feeding regularly. The hunters set out on the five-hour drive to the game reserve.

Long hours had passed in the blind and there had been no sign of the cat. At dusk, Dirk scanned the low thorns and grass for any sign that the leopard had returned. His eyes kept going back to the long, crooked branch where the bait hung. With daylight fading and no sign of the cat, the hunt would have to be put off until morning if the leopard did not show itself in the next few minutes. Then, as silently as the creeping shadows that stretched across the sand, the cat appeared. Dirk motioned to Donna to be ready and they watched as the leopard—a big, heavy male with a thick neck and a gorgeous, dappled coat that glistened in the dying light of day—slipped up into the tree and stood silhouetted above the half-eaten remains of the bait.

Donna shifted silently forward, pressed her face against the stock, and found the cat in the scope of her rifle. She focused on the shoulder, settled the cross hairs on a single rosette, and pressed the trigger. The evening erupted in a flash of flame as the thunderous report of the rifle echoed out across the plains, rolling into the distance as the leopard slumped and fell dead at the base of the tree.

Back at Onguma there was a great deal of celebration over the taking of the grand old tom, an excellent trophy and one of Africa's most difficult prizes. The Boddingtons and Dirk sat around the fire with the owner of the game reserve under a belt of glossy white stars, drinking wine and eating as Donna relived her experience for them. Her story took her listeners through the long hours of late afternoon to the moment when she centered her sights on the cat, and ended with that final walk up to the dead tom lying outstretched at the foot of the tree.

Le Roux, the owner of Onguma, turned to Craig and said he had some good news from the government regarding the hunting of lions on Onguma's vast acreage. Unlike many areas in Africa where lion numbers were rapidly decreasing, the number of cats at Onguma was on the increase, causing conflict with locals. The result was that Le Roux had been awarded an exceedingly rare problem-lion permit, one of less than a dozen or so that are given out annually across the country. Problem-lion permits are available only when the government deems a cat to be a serious risk to life or property, and the issuance of a problem-lion tag for Onguma indicated that a lion had created a real nuisance in the region. In the firelight, Le Roux leaned over toward Craig and asked if he would be interested in taking a lion on Onguma.

Night falls over Etosha and the silent sentinels keep watch for lions. **(Photo courtesy of Jacques Strauss)**

"Of course," was Craig's easy reply, and they began to plan their lion hunt by the dim light of the crackling fire. The decision was made to set out at dawn and look for tracks. PH Danny Bartlett and Dirk would accompany Craig and help him search for the big male in the thorn and acacia forests of Onguma. Craig's rifle was a left-handed .300 Remington Ultra Magnum—certainly enough gun for any lion and within the legal limit for lion calibers in Namibia, but not Craig's first choice for a dedicated lion hunt. Danny offered Craig a right-handed .375 Brno, but Craig, more familiar with his .300, chose to stay with the rifle that he knew well.

With limited time available, the hunters would have to rely on Danny's and Le Roux's knowledge of the lions on Onguma and hope to find the big cat quickly. Lions, particularly males, roam over vast areas, and older males that have been ousted from their pride may cover many miles in search of food or new territory. It would be difficult to find the big male and put it in the salt with so little time remaining in the safari. When the morning light turned the plains a steely gray, and while the embers of the previous night's fire smoldered in the gray ash pit, the hunters set out in search of the nuisance lion.

The hunters came up empty-handed. The only lion spoor that they came across early that first morning belonged to lionesses with cubs. Even these tracks were old, and by midday the group still hadn't found a footprint; they saw no signs of the big male in the area. That afternoon, however, they drove out to a remote water hole, and as Dirk walked the perimeter of the pan, he came across a massive set of pug marks cut cleanly in the loose sand. This was the lion they were after.

Dirk and the others wasted no time in securing a kudu cow for bait, hanging the carcass and clearing a path so that they could slip in to view the kudu bait from the blind without having to negotiate a minefield of broken branches and brittle leaves. If the lion heard anything, it might well leave the area, never to return. As the sun sank and the western sky turned a familiar shade of deep red, the hunters activated an electronic lion call in hopes that the cat was within earshot. There was no more to do at that point, other than wait.

They climbed into the hunting truck and headed back for camp, each contemplating the possibility of a showdown with a lion in the morning hours. As the group made its way back toward Onguma Lodge, they came upon three young male lions lying outstretched in the sand, their short, light manes growing tight against their heads. The cats all turned and focused their eyes on the approaching truck, affording it a casual glance as they rested in the warm desert sand. In a few hours these cats would be on patrol, slipping through the blackness as they searched for game. But during the last lingering moments of daylight the cats were satisfied to simply lie in the cover of the thorns, blinking at the truck and the hunters until the motor hummed and the truck slipped away from the trio of cats and back toward Onguma.

That night, the hunters sat in the warm glow of the firelight knowing full well that out on the dark plains, beside the remote water hole that glistened silver in the moonlight, the old lion might be feeding on their kudu offering. The anticipation of the hunt peaked when Dirk, Craig, and Danny rose well before dawn to see if the lion had taken the bait.

It was still not fully daylight when the hunters reached the water hole. In the chill of early morning, Dirk and Craig set off down the cleaned path to the blind, stepping quietly and trying to prepare themselves for the very real possibility that the big lion was feeding just ahead in the dim light. But such was not the case. When Dirk saw that there were no lions, he and Craig had a chance to relax and look over the bait.

The kudu remained intact and untouched, except for the growing cloud of metallic-green Calliphoridae bottle flies that took up residence on the carcass after the sun rose. Dirk walked around the bait and was shocked to see a fresh set of prints left by the big male from the night before. The cat had come to the bait and, for reasons unknown, had simply walked past it without stopping to feed.

Danny told the others that the lion they were hunting had recently lost its pride. The old male was most likely crossing through the area in search of its lost harem of lionesses and had simply passed by the kudu on its search to reclaim its lost females. The good news, however, was that the lion was still in the area and that it frequented the water hole. As the cool morning gave way to the sun and heat of midday, there was little use in staying at the blind. The cat would, in all likelihood, find a cool place to spend the long, hot afternoon. The hunters decided to do the same and planned to return later to set up for the evening's hunt.

When the hunters returned that evening, the lion had still not come to the bait. Only the legions of flies worked on the kudu. Daylight faded and the evening sun cast long shadows on the sandy earth around the water hole. The lion now knew that the kudu was near the water hole, and, with luck, it would give in to hunger and come to feed that night. Craig and Dirk stood beside the truck in the late hours of the day, talking quietly and planning their next move. Dirk pulled out the electronic caller and began filling the bush with the sounds of a lion roaring.

Almost immediately, the call was answered.

Dirk and Craig stood in astonishment as the sound of the electronic roar rolled out over the plains and, even before the last resonating echoes faded, was met by the gravelly challenge of a big male lion. The cat's voice swelled over the plains, chilling the hunters' blood as they listened to the lion give a series of raspy roars and then a series of shorter grunts as a challenge to the electronic call.

Dirk and Craig waited for five tense minutes, listening to the silence that surrounded them. Dirk turned the call back on. Once again the digital lion gave voice, and its challenge was immediately met by the voice of the real thing, a big male lion looking for its pride and boiling for a fight. The roars came again, this time closer and more forceful.

"He's coming," Dirk said.

Craig's big lion. (Photo courtesy of Craig Boddington)

The big cat was headed back toward the water hole, looking to rendezvous with the other lion. From the sound of its roaring, the old lion was coming in a hurry and would be aggressive and ready for battle when it arrived.

Dirk, Danny, and Craig slipped back down the trail to the blind and were there only a short time before the lion appeared, holding its head high, its massive body dark against the light grass. There was no question that this scarred veteran was the lion they were after, the ousted ruler of the local pride that intended to fight its way back to power. The lion broke out of the heavy thorn forty yards from the men and paused, turning its attention immediately toward the blind.

Craig knew it was time and stepped into position, lifting his .300 Remington Ultra Magnum to his shoulder and letting the cross hairs settle over the vitals. When his aim felt right, he pressed the trigger. A scorching flash of flame leapt from the barrel and the lion rose up, hit hard, and roared as it somersaulted. Once the cat regained its feet, it broke into a run and headed directly for the blind, covering the earth in great bounds. The rifles rang again, Danny firing a round from his .375 H&H that missed the tumbling, roaring cat, and Craig firing again into the oncoming cat, the 200-grain Swift A-Frame hitting squarely in the center of the lion's chest and turning it. As the bullet crashed home, the lion broke off the charge and headed parallel to the blind, collapsing not more than forty yards away.

"Leave it," Dirk said, his own rifle leveled and ready for a shot. Over the iron sights of his rifle, Dirk watched as the lion breathed its last. Craig's shots had been true.

When they found that the lion was down for good, Craig and Dirk examined it in the fading light. It was a huge, old lion with a spider's web of scars across its muzzle. Dirk immediately recognized that this was a tremendous cat. Later, he discovered it would rank as the new Namibian number one. With the cat loaded in the truck, the men headed back to camp under the silver light of the stars, toward the celebration that awaited them after a successful hunt for Africa's single greatest trophy, a big male lion.

CHAPTER 26

A Curious Nature

Professional hunter: Reinhard Mosich
Location: Erongo Mountains

It was going to be a cold, uncomfortable night of waiting in the leopard blind. The leopard had dragged the bait to the center of a rock cathedral high in the jagged peaks, and since there was very little cover available to build a blind, Reinhard Mosich of Kuduberg Safaris had decided the best option was to hide among the granite rock piles surrounding the bait. The spoor indicated that the leopard was a large tom, and it was obviously comfortable among the rocks, even if Reinhard and his client were not. Client and PH sat together amid the high rock walls, adjusting their positions now and then to try to find a less uncomfortable place to sit. A long, thin sliver of the moon was visible in a cleft between two rocks above the men.

The best option to take the cat, as Reinhard saw it, was to settle in the rocks near the bait and drape camouflage netting over the top of the rocks. This would allow the men to move for a shot without letting the old cat know they were there. Behind the makeshift blind was a large boulder that served as a cold and uncomfortable cushion for Reinhard and his client to lean against as they settled in to wait through the night, hoping that the leopard would come in to feed at dawn.

Long into the night, Reinhard stayed awake and watched the narrow channel of night sky that was visible between two rocks. A vibrant collection of stars glimmered in the sky above, glistening in the clean desert air. Off to the right, the deep blue glow of the moon was still visible in the sky, although the moon itself was hidden behind one of the spires of rock. It was a cold night even for the Namibian winter, and Reinhard pulled his arms across his chest to warm himself against the chill of the desert night.

There was no sound for six hours except the chattering cry of distant jackals and the echoing whine of an owl calling down the canyon walls.

Zebra herd moving at sunset. (Photo courtesy of Jofie Lamprecht)

Then, after midnight, Reinhard heard the shuffling of feet on the smooth rocks ahead of them. In the dim light he could make out the forms of two animals as they moved over the rocks, a pair of dark shadows that slowly changed position in the blue light.

A sudden crack of bone breaking between heavy jaws gave Reinhard a start. He leaned over to his client, who had somehow managed to find a suitable position for sleep, and gently shook him. When his client's head lifted, Reinhard shushed him and nodded toward the bait. By then the darkness was filled with the sounds of feasting. Reinhard lifted a big electric light that was beside his leg and, pointing it toward the bait, pressed the button. There was a mechanical click and then a solid beam of white light shone into the rocks ahead.

"What are they?" his client asked.

In the circle of light several shaggy brown forms stopped feeding and stood staring up at the men in silence, their unblinking eyes shining white in the beam of light.

"Brown hyenas," Reinhard said to his client. "A whole family."

Brown hyena sightings are rare in Africa, with the majority of these animals living in arid and semiarid regions of Namibia, including the Kalahari and Namib Deserts. *Hyaena brunnea,* as the brown hyena is known to science, is slightly smaller than its relative, the spotted hyena. Brown hyenas also live in much smaller social groups than their larger cousins and, unlike spotted hyenas, are largely scavengers, feeding on the leftover kills of lions, leopards, wild dogs, and other hyenas as well as on fruits and vegetables, insects, and occasional small mammals.

Reinhard and his client watched the clan as the hyena family shuffled around the kill in the darkness, pulling meat from the carcass in strips and cracking bones with their powerful jaws. After some time, Reinhard heard a curious sound on the rocks behind them—a faint padding against the stone face, like bare feet walking over the rocks. The sound came again, faint and low in the stillness of the night—a sound that would have been inaudible among the chatter of birds and

Scouting for game. (Photo courtesy of Benjamin and Veronica Gettinger)

the hum of insects at midday. Slowly, the animal made its way to just beyond the thin camouflage netting.

Reinhard listened as the animal sniffed at the netting. The top of the blind shifted, and slowly, ever so slowly, Reinhard turned in the darkness to face the animal that had entered the blind behind him. He pressed the switch on the spotlight, and there, blinking against the sudden flash of light, was the hyena matriarch. Its shaggy face and large, round ears were inside the top of the blind, four feet above and behind the men. It blinked again at the light, testing the air inside the blind and examining the two men sitting just before it.

Then, without haste or concern, the hyena pulled its head out of the blind and softly padded back down the rock face, apparently unalarmed at the presence of the men. It walked to the front of the blind and touched its nose to the netting, showing neither fear nor aggression. Eventually its curiosity was satisfied and it turned, shuffling back to the others, and took its place at the carcass. The hyenas fed for some time, and then the clan began to move silently back into the shadows cast by the moonlight on the rocks.

Reinhard vividly remembers the events and the emotion he felt at the matriarch's appearance: the tense sensation of knowing that something had entered the blind, and the enjoyment of trading long glances with the hyena as it examined them sitting in the blind. It was a simple exchange between two species that happened to meet one night in the darkness of the Erongo Mountains.

African animals have a well-documented reputation for being tough and resisting death. But one of the traits of African game that is perhaps not as well known is its intense curiosity. Often hunters can use this characteristic to their advantage to take a shot at a moment of hesitation by a curious animal.

Reinhard's encounter with the hyena would be his closest interaction with a wild animal up to that point, but that would change when he and his client spent an afternoon hunting kudus in the Erongos.

Lilac-breasted roller, one of Namibia's most colorful birds. (Photo courtesy of Jacques Strauss)

The steep, granite cliffs of the Erongos make it impossible to drive vehicles into the most rugged portions of the range, but the overhangs and rock piles make excellent vantage points for observing game as it moves through the valleys late in the evening. Reinhard and his client were seated along a path leading up a ridge, examining a bachelor herd of kudu bulls that contained several males of questionable trophy quality. They decided to pass on the bulls, hoping to find something larger, and so they spent the late hours of the winter afternoon contentedly watching the bulls feeding out of the draw. Because the plan was to watch for game from vantage points above the valley, Reinhard had brought his terrier, Beppi, along. Beppi took full advantage of the afternoon sun and stretched out at full length on the warm earth near Reinhard's boots.

As they watched the kudu bulls, Reinhard saw a herd of Hartmann zebras walking along a trail on the valley floor. Like all zebras, the Hartmann variety is normally extremely wary. Reinhard's attention turned to the zebra herd, which was being led by its dominant mare up the same trail where Reinhard and his client were seated. The hunters leaned back against the rocks and waited for the herd of seven zebras to catch their scent and run.

Unlike most prey animals, which have a wide field of view but rather limited acuity, zebras reputedly have the ability to pick out objects against a background. This adds to the difficulty when planning a stalk, but the band of zebras approaching Reinhard seemed unconcerned, despite the lead mare's intense gaze. The mare stood with its head high, testing the wind.

After a few moments it approached the men, its head down, nostrils flaring, moving closer until its muzzle was near Reinhard's knee. The potential gravity of the situation occurred to Reinhard, who suddenly realized that he and his client were very close to a very powerful wild animal and that the rock face behind them prevented their escape. The mare blinked at Reinhard, reaching down to sniff his knee.

Beppi raised his head, and for a moment Reinhard feared that the dog would frighten the zebra, which could in turn bite or kick. But neither

Beppi nor the mare seemed inclined to fight. Instead, Beppi looked up at the zebra's pulsing black muzzle as the mare sniffed Reinhard's knee. The band of zebras surrounded the men, waiting for the lead mare's response. Reinhard could smell the warm barnyard smell of the mare, a familiar scent to anyone who has been around horses.

Seemingly satisfied, the mare turned and led its band up the trail, hoofs clanking on the loose rocks as they moved into heavy cover and out of sight. During its lifetime the mare had surely smelled man, and if it associated the human scent with danger it certainly showed no indications that it perceived Reinhard's scent as a sign of possible peril. Perhaps it was Beppi's presence that confused the old mare, or, perhaps just as likely, it had simply acted on its curiosity and explored something that was unique in its environment. This sensitivity seems of special relevance to hunters since curiosity and exploration are key elements in the satisfaction of a day spent afield.

CHAPTER 27

LIGHTNING

Professional hunter: Elaine Coetzee
Location: Central Plateau

In the hours just before dawn, Elaine Coetzee of CEC Safaris and her client sat at the breakfast table at the lodge and discussed the difficulties of hunting a cheetah, a cat that is not only the world's fastest, but one of the most difficult to hunt.

"They are not like other cats," Elaine explained as they drank coffee in the still of predawn.

"We have plenty of cheetahs here," Elaine continued. "But pure luck plays a big role in taking one. You cannot bait them. They won't eat rotten meat. You can only sit at a play tree and wait, or ambush them on foot. The odds of catching a cheetah, however, especially a big male, at a play tree during daylight hours are very slim."

Nevertheless, Elaine's client wanted to take a big male cheetah, and, as luck would have it, Elaine and her husband (CEC co-owner Cornie Coetzee, himself a well-respected Namibian PH) had found the spoor of a pair of large male cheetahs that had entered their hunting concession three days earlier. Since cheetahs are largely nomadic and often do not have well-defined home ranges, it was likely that the two males would roam through the CEC concession, killing game and looking for females, until they decided to move on to other parts. Their stay in the concession could last weeks or hours. That was one of the difficulties of hunting cheetahs.

Determined to find her client a good cat, Elaine loaded the hunting truck. As the sun rose over the distant rocky hilltops, the truck was bouncing over a sandy two-track road near the perimeter of the hunting concession. With her client beside her and their tracker in the back, Elaine toiled along with the truck in low gear, watching the red sand on either side of the road for any cheetah tracks.

Recent rains had pummeled the concession, and the normally short-cropped plains were a sea of waist-high grass that was still green

Kalahari rainstorm. (Photo courtesy of Jofie Lamprecht)

and thick after the months of steady precipitation. The forests of camelthorn acacia and thornbush were also green with new growth, and the entire landscape was overrun with heavy vegetation—a rarity during the Namibian hunting season. The thick foliage would make it very difficult for the hunters to see the cats until they were very close. By then, it would likely be too late.

Elaine caught sight of something beside the road and pressed the brake of the hunting truck. On the side of the two-track road, pressed deep into the moist sand, were the tracks of two male cheetahs leaving the concession. Elaine's heart sank. The odds of these prints

belonging to another pair of cats was slim, and it was clear that the cheetahs had crossed the boundary of the concession, perhaps never to be seen again.

But such was not the case.

Only a little farther down the road, the spoor of the two males reappeared. The cheetahs had, for reasons unknown, returned to the CEC hunting area after briefly venturing away. This spoor appeared very fresh as well. Odds were that the two males were still in the concession. Still, that meant that the cats could be anywhere among several thousand acres of dense green vegetation, and even if the hunters saw the cats, they would likely see only their heads bouncing above the wall of grass. Elaine and her crew continued on the roads for several hours, looking for any sign of the two male cheetahs. When noon came and they had still not seen any sign of the cats, the hunting party returned to the lodge for lunch.

By the time they had finished lunch, the sky had darkened and grim storm clouds rose like a black anvil in the sky to the north. Distant flashes of lightning illuminated the base of the storm, and the rumbling of thunder could be heard even over the dull drone of the truck motor as the hunters continued their search. If they didn't get a break before the storm clouds reached them, they would have to give up for the day. And that meant they wouldn't be able to hunt until the following morning, and who knew where the cheetahs would likely be by that time. The crew was going to need a lucky break very soon or their opportunity would be lost for good.

Suddenly Elaine heard a series of hard thumps against the roof of the hunting vehicle. Her tracker, who was riding in the safari seat in the back, said he had seen two cheetahs sitting under a camelthorn acacia a quarter-mile away. Elaine stopped the truck and motioned for her client to get out, explaining that if he wanted his cat, he was going to have to act quickly.

The northern sky was a shade of deep, steely gray when Elaine and her client started across the plain toward the lonely acacia tree where the cheetahs had taken refuge. They moved forward on hands and knees, Elaine keeping an eye out for snakes as they moved through the tall grass, which rippled like ocean waves in the wind generated by the coming storm. On occasion, Elaine would risk a glance above the grass to check on the cats. Seeing the outlines of the two cats sitting just where they had been earlier, she continued forward with the shooting sticks clutched in her hand and her client following close behind her.

The rush of spring growth had resulted in an abundance of pollen in the grasses. As Elaine and her client moved forward through the grass, the pollen began to stir Elaine's allergies. She stopped, blinking away the tears in her eyes and trying to breathe in air that was not contaminated by the pollen grains. But it was impossible. The cloud of pollen that hung around the two hunters would be her undoing. Finally, she could take no more. She braced herself, fighting against the urge

Hunting cheetahs is never easy. The cats usually won't come to bait, and they move continually throughout their territory. Taking a good cheetah requires patience, persistence, and luck. (Photo courtesy of Benjamin Gettinger)

The day after the storm, Elaine and her client pose with their hard-earned trophy. The big male cheetah nearly eluded the hunters. (Photo courtesy of Elaine Coetzee)

to sneeze. It came again, a horrible, powerless feeling. Elaine fought as best she could and held it off. But she knew she could not hold out for long. Sooner or later the pollen would get the best of her.

"You have to shoot now," she said, turning to her client. "I'm going to sneeze, and if that happens, they will be gone. You can do it."

The range was just about three hundred yards, and the males sat where they had been, just under the wide-reaching branches of the camelthorn tree that stood alone in a sea of grass and thorn. Elaine set up the shooting sticks and her client rose up to his knees, resting his rifle and pausing just long enough to align the sights before pressing the trigger. The report of the rifle was like a thunderclap, and Elaine saw the biggest male flip over backward before rising and disappearing into the tall grass.

"We have to try to find that cat as soon as we can," Elaine said, wiping tears from her eyes and thankful to be standing upright, away from the grass. Client and PH headed forward quickly, stopping at the base of the camelthorn tree, where a spattering of blood was scattered over the flattened grass.

By that time, the storm was almost on top of the hunters and the wind was high. In the distance, white bolts of lightning reached down toward the rocky hills. If the storm washed away the blood spoor and the cat continued moving, there was almost no chance that they would ever find the cheetah again.

"Go get Snippie," Elaine said to her tracker. The tracker nodded and turned, heading back to the truck at a jog. Snippie, her terrier, would root out the cat, and she could work much faster following the scent trail than the hunters could by following the visible clues left behind by the running cheetah. The tracker returned from the truck with the excited terrier tucked under his arm just as the first fat drops of rain hit the sand and swelled in the dry earth.

Snippie wasted little time figuring out the cat's trail, and as the rain began to fall in earnest, the group followed the little dog. Soon the black storm clouds released a deluge that roared down on the green plain, punctuated now and again by a brilliant flash of lightning or the rumble and boom of thunder that shook the wet earth. Snippie never faltered.

Suddenly the terrier stopped on the perimeter of a large thornbush, barking into the sheets of rain and wind as she worked in a half-circle around the overgrown thorns. Elaine shielded her face from the driving rain and heard a deep snarl come from within the twisted arms of the thorn. There, pressed deep in the tangles, stood a massive male cheetah. It growled at the dog, which stood on the outer edge of the bush, barking and trembling.

"Finish the cat," Elaine said. Her client raised his rifle and shot once more. The bullet struck home and the cheetah slumped down, dead.

The worst of the storm had passed. The savanna began to absorb the standing water as the gloom began to fade. Elaine and her client pulled the big male cheetah from the bush, marveling at its immense size and heft. It was by far the largest cheetah that Elaine had ever seen. As Snippie bounded around the client's heels, Elaine and her tracker hoisted the cheetah onto the client's shoulders. They posed together for a photo as the last of the rain clouds broke up, and the echo of backslaps and congratulations blended with the distant drumming of departing thunder.

The hunters returned to camp, soaked and happy. After showers and a meal, the hunters sat around the fire with sundowners in hand and celebrated their success. Elaine knew that the cheetah was large, but she could not have imagined that the cat would turn out to be the new world record, besting the old record by more than a centimeter of skull length. Best of all, they had earned it, hunting on foot and following their trophy into the heart of the storm.

CHAPTER 28

THE DRY SPELL

Professional hunter: Roger Coomber
Location: Damaraland

Roger Coomber and his companions squatted beside a sandy path and studied the elephant prints, as big as beach balls and pressed so deeply into the powdery Damaraland sand that the individual lines and bifurcations on each foot left a mark in the earth like a fingerprint. Finding these prints was laced with irony since Roger and the others were not simply looking for any bull elephant. The men were after an individual rogue with a record of attacking the Damara people and ransacking their villages and farms. The print of the big elephant bull pressed into the brittle white sand might just lead the men to the outlaw they were searching for. If Roger and the others could find the bull, they could put an end to his months of destruction.

It was the winter of 2007, one of the driest years on record in Namibia. Namibian game animals are astoundingly well adapted to live in an arid environment that receives very little rainfall throughout the year, but prolonged periods without any rain at all can have devastating effects on the country's wildlife, just as heavy snow can cause great die-offs in winter deer yards in the northern United States. The game in Damaraland had been suffering without water for some time, and many of the animals had moved out of their traditional range in northwestern Namibia and into towns such as Kamanjab. In particular, a group of elephants had been terrorizing villages and farms, knocking down windmills, ripping up pipes, shattering the walls of reservoirs, and wreaking havoc in their mad search for water.

As the drought continued, more and more elephants destroyed property in the areas around Damaraland. Eventually the problem became so severe that the Loxodonta Africana Conservancy in Damaraland was granted two special problem-animal control permits from the Namibian Ministry of Environment and Tourism, which allowed for the killing and export of two specific rogue elephants in the region that had proven extremely destructive and dangerous. Roger Coomber's Vieranas Safaris, a member of the Loxodonta Africana Conservancy, was allocated one of these permits. This was, in large part, because the elephants that were driven out of Damaraland traveled down the corridors of the Ugab, Kalkfeld, and Kamanjab Rivers onto private land, many of them crossing through hunting areas under the control of Vieranas Safaris.

Roger brought in another guide who was certified in Namibia to hunt dangerous game. NAPHA, the professional organization of Namibian hunters, has set certain guidelines as to which PHs are certified to hunt certain species or in certain areas. Only hunters certified to hunt dangerous game can pursue elephants, and, at the time, Coomber did not have the certification needed and had to ask an additional PH to help him destroy the bull. The danger posed by this particular rogue bull warranted an extra set of eyes and another big gun, anyway.

After the control permit was issued for the elephant, Roger had to drive several hours south to pick up his German friend and client, Jochen, as well as Jochen's wife, Ute, and his hunting companion, Egon. With the PAC permit in hand, the elephant was fully exportable as a trophy. It was not only a good opportunity for Jochen to take a bull but it would also help out the local community at the same time. After returning to the Vieranas camp, the new arrivals were treated to dinner, drinks, and conversation around the braai. The hunters thought about the coming days while they sat around the dying curls of orange camelthorn embers, looking up from the flames now and then at the belt of stars overhead and listening to the sounds of the night animals that moved just beyond the far edge of the firelight.

The elephant hunt started the following morning just after breakfast. Jochen pulled his .458 Lott rifle from its case, opened the bolt, and began feeding the massive cartridges into the magazine. Roger's men set a target downrange and beat a hasty retreat as Jochen settled down

Dust devil during Namibia's dry season. (Photo by Benjamin and Veronica Gettinger)

behind the express iron sights of the Lott, centered the front bead just below the middle of the target, and touched off a round. The still of morning was broken as the great rifle cracked. Roger worked the bolt, found center again, and let another 500-grain slug rip through the target downrange. The finger-size holes in the target had been punched within an inch of one another. It was time to hunt an elephant.

It wasn't hard to track the bull's movements around the farms and villages near the border of Damaraland. The bull had demolished water pumps and broken through fences on a rampage from one village to the next. On several occasions, farmers and workers had been subjected to the bull's ill temper, and there had been several narrow escapes. It was only a matter of time before someone crossed the bull and wasn't lucky enough to escape its wrath.

Elephants use water for drinking and to protect their skin from the African sun. As water supplies

The hunting car rolled to a stop in a swirl of white, powdery dust, and the group stepped out to speak with local farmers who had seen the bull the night before. The farmer had posted one of his men high on a ridge where they had seen the bull passing the previous day. Upon finding the man and the tracks, Roger and the others set out in search of the bull, which had climbed up the ridge before breaking over the top and heading down into the valley on the opposite side. With any luck, they would find the crop raider there.

They backed up the truck and steered a course that would lead around the base of a large stone outcropping the bull had crossed. Far down on the opposite side was the dirt road that led to the farm.

dwindle, elephants become increasingly desperate. (Photo courtesy of Gerard Erasmus)

The men decided to make their way down to the plains in hopes of intersecting the bull's track as it crossed through the farmland. But it was to no avail. The bull seemed to have vanished.

On Monday morning, Roger received a call from another local farmer who had cut the spoor of a bull elephant. With his men and rifles loaded in the hunting vehicle, Roger headed toward the farm. It didn't take them long to find the tracks of a bull mixed in with a herd that had moved across the farm in search of water. With their water bags filled and their heavy rifles propped over their shoulders, the men set out in single file through the gray clumps of wait-a-bit thorn and scattered acacia trees, stopping periodically to scan the terrain ahead for any sign of the bull.

Elephants generally avoid contact with humans. However, periods of extended drought cause elephant herds to come into conflict with humans. (Photo courtesy of Jacques Strauss)

For two hours the hunting party followed the spoor, finally catching sight of a patch of wrinkled, gray elephant hide, the rolling slope of a shoulder, and the fanning of an ear in the thornbush ahead of them. After careful examination, they determined that the bull standing with the mixed group of cows, adolescent bulls, and calves was not the one they wanted. A young bull caught wind of the men and spooked, alarming the matriarch, which turned, ears fanned, and sounded the alarm before leading the herd away in a veil of dust.

On the third morning of the hunt, another farmer within the conservancy called Roger and told him that the bull was on his farm, that it was with another big bull, and that two of his men were out in the bush keeping track of them. It was great news, and the frustrations of the previous two days melted away with the heat of the rising sun. Roger gathered the others, who quickly ate their breakfasts while pulling on boots and packing their rifles and jackets into the steel bed of the pickup. When the last of the gear was loaded, they set out to find the offending elephant.

Just as the farmer had promised, his men had dogged the bulls, keeping them in view until Roger and the others arrived with their heavy rifles. Taking their gear in hand and guzzling a last drink from the water bags, the men set out, moving low and close together toward the two massive gray bulls that loomed larger with each carefully placed footstep.

There was no escaping the devil thorns that hooked and held the men. Each time they snagged a bush jacket or pant leg, the brittle thorns made an unnerving scraping sound that caused the group to freeze and watch the bulls ahead, waiting for a sign of widespread ears or uplifted trunk that meant that their stalk was blown.

Finally the men crouched at the edge of a circle of trees and dusty gray thorn that hid the bulls just ahead of them. As they prepared to close the gap and get into position for the killing shot, Roger felt the cool, dry wind creeping across his neck. The men turned back, and together they moved quickly away, barely managing to keep their scent away from the bulls. When the wind settled, the men moved forward once again, closing the gap and entering the big rogue's personal space, watching as it fed just ahead of them. *My lord,* Roger thought, *if it knew we were here. . . .*

Just then, the PH who was assisting Roger got the men's attention and motioned toward the second bull, which was equally as large as the rogue and perhaps of the same ill humor. It was standing in a Terminalia thicket at two o'clock to their position. Now the men had two big bulls to contend with, and they had no idea what the second bull would do when they shot the first.

Roger set up the shooting sticks, and Jochen let the rifle settle into position. The rogue had turned perpendicular to the hunting party, its great, gray body rising high above the Terminalia as its huge ears fanned like two tattered sails on a great ship. Jochen centered the wide express sights of the .458 Lott on a spot a finger's length ahead of the opening of the ear. If his shot was true, the 500-grain slug would drive its way through the matrix of honeycomb caverns in the elephant's skull and reach the brain.

Jochen pressed the trigger and the rifle rose up from the sticks with a tremendous crash. The rogue collapsed just ahead of them, its six tons of mass splintering the Terminalia around it and raising a cloud of dust as it fell in a great heap so close to the men that they felt the shuddering earth under their leather boots. But there was no time for Roger, Jochen, and the others to admire the elephant. As the first bull fell, the second roared and spun toward the men, swallowing the narrow space between them in two great strides. Jochen quickly fired a shot that passed just over the bull's head, turning it and sending it off in a stiff-legged run. As the men scanned the thicket over the sights of their rifles, they listened to the thrashing sounds of the second bull charging through the thicket.

Roger and the others moved slowly up to the dead rogue, tossing rocks and waiting to be sure that the bull was, indeed, dead and not simply stunned. When they had satisfied themselves that the bull was well and truly dead, the men began offering congratulations to Jochen on taking the old rogue at such close range.

It was late by this time, so they decided to head back to the farm and wait for morning to bring a crew and trucks to begin the process of butchering and distributing meat from the elephant. The farmer was elated to hear that the old bull that had destroyed his water tanks was out of commission. Best of all, they had managed to take the bull without having to kill its old compadre.

Old Namibian bull. (Photo courtesy of Jofie Lamprecht)

All celebration ended at dawn, as the men stood in front of the truck and looked down upon a massive set of very fresh elephant tracks leading back to the carcass of the dead rogue. Its companion had returned to the area after the men had left in an apparent effort to find its fallen comrade. That meant that the second bull would almost certainly be in a deadly mood, and if the men came upon it, there was a better-than-average chance the elephant would try to settle the score for its pal.

Slowly the men approached the downed bull, walking in the fresh tracks of the second bull, which was headed in the same direction. The men stopped every few strides and scanned the elephant-colored thorn and acacia for any sign of the second bull, but there was none. It seemed the second bull had come back, found its companion dead, and then had continued on its way.

The crew began the tremendous task of skinning and butchering the great bull, a task that had to be completed entirely in the field while trucks ferried the meat to households around Kamanjab. Roger and his men loaded their truck with great red elephant steaks and took them to the local school, where the children watched with anticipation as the men unloaded the meat that would feed them for weeks. The bull, once a liability to the residents of Kamanjab, was now providing them with much-needed protein to see them through the remainder of the drought. When the rains came at last and the grass of the Damara Plains once again turned green, the elephants disappeared back into the rocky hills, vanishing from the valley where the old rogue had fallen.

CHAPTER 29

The Veteran

Professional hunter: Jofie Lamprecht
Location: Waterberg Plateau

It was midday high on the Waterberg Plateau. The long shadows of morning had grown shorter with the rising of the sun. Jofie Lamprecht, barely thirty years old but already a seasoned professional hunter, sat still and silent on a column of red rocks. Through his field glasses, he studied the dim canyon below him, a scattered mix of jade-colored foliage and rusty-red stone. It wasn't long before Jofie found what he was searching for. He leaned back against the rock and watched as the hulking gray body of a rhinoceros bull slipped silently out of the thorn a hundred yards below. For the next twenty minutes, Jofie watched the bull working its way down through the rocks. It is an old bull, Jofie thought. A spider's web of both fresh and aged scars were scattered across its broad, clay-colored face. There was little doubt that this was the bull Jofie was looking for. He recognized it by the fact that its second horn was missing; it had been severed in a fight with another rhino.

The old bull was an exceptional trophy even though it had only a single horn. The only problem was that Jofie, who sat in the growing heat watching the bull wander across the valley floor below, did not have a client in camp with a license to hunt rhino. All Jofie could do was to stretch out on the smooth surface of the rocks, the scent of blooming acacia heavy in the air, and watch the battle-tested bull as it fed across the valley.

It was not long, however, before Jofie did have a client arrive who possessed a coveted rhino tag. His client, who was seventy-two years old, had been offered a unique opportunity to hunt the most specialized of all the Big Five. The white rhino, thanks in large part to dedicated conservation efforts funded largely by sport hunters, can be hunted on a limited basis in Namibia, but it is the most specialized and expensive of all of the Big Five to collect. Jofie had been fortunate enough to hunt rhinos in the past and had an understanding of what was required to hunt these prehistoric-

White rhinos were once on the brink of extinction, but today they are found in huntable numbers in Namibia and South Africa. **(Photo courtesy of Jofie Lamprecht)**

looking beasts successfully. But all the rhinos he had hunted had been in enclosures where only a select group of trophy rhinos could be harvested. Never had he led a safari in search of a completely wild rhino that lived in an unfenced area.

Jofie made the long drive from the Waterberg down Namibia's main stretch of paved highway toward Windhoek and on to the international airport. He fetched his client and offered him encouraging news: There was a rhino bull in the area, and the odds of taking it were high since Jofie had patterned the old rhino and had a good idea of where to find the bull.

The Waterberg Plateau is a great massif that rises high above the surrounding veld. The topography and ecosystem of the Waterberg is entirely different from that of the surrounding plains, which lie six hundred feet below the summit of the plateau. High, red stone cliffs separate the plains from the plateau. Once designated as a park for the reintroduction of the Cape eland, the Waterberg is now a flourishing game park that is home to black and white rhinos, Cape buffaloes, elands, roans, sables, and other species. The Lamprecht family controlled the hunting on the plateau. Under the careful governance of the Lamprechts there was minimal hunting pressure, so the Waterberg had become one of Africa's most exclusive safari destinations, a place where trophies grew old and large.

Much of Africa's rhino hunting takes place on private farms and game reserves where rhinos are introduced and monitored. Hunters may only have a chance at a single bull or two deemed huntable by the landowner and the government. Such is not the case on the Waterberg, where rhinos have ranged freely since their reintroduction many years ago. The natural border of the park and the vastness of the plateau allow rhinos to live freely and without pressure from man. Rhino hunting on the Waterberg today is done much the way it was in the early twentieth century. The hunters find tracks, follow the spoor, and hope to get a chance for a shot at a good bull.

Jofie had been following the single-horned bull's odd-shaped, three-toed prints since early morning. Scattered along the spoor were pools of dank urine soaking into the red sand and dung piles that served as markers to alert other bulls that the old rhino had claimed this portion of the Waterberg as its own. Since Hunters Namibia had taken control of hunting operations in 2009, Jofie had spent long days traveling across the plateau on foot and in his hunting vehicle. He had walked many dusty miles on the tracks of rhinos and had seen several good bulls, but none that matched the character of this old, one-horned, four-ton veteran, a brute among brutes. When Jofie saw the territorial sign and the deep spoor, he recognized the mark of the old veteran at once. Seven miles later, Jofie and the game scouts that accompanied him found the bull moving through the same valley where Jofie had first seen it, its inch-thick armored skin mottled gray and red from the Waterberg sand.

The game scouts had to conclude that the rhino was indeed an old, mature bull before they would allow Jofie to hunt it. At first sight, the game rangers agreed that the old rhino with the single horn was indeed a trophy worth taking. Jofie and the others watched as the bull moved down the valley, its wide head swaying as it walked, and disappeared into the thornscrub.

Jofie's client, a man from Holland, was back at camp waiting for news about the rhino. Because of his client's age, Jofie had decided to locate the rhino first before setting his client forth on the track. The vastness of the Waterberg meant that the rhino might wander for miles through the sand and hills. Jofie and the others had seen the old rhino trundle down the length of the valley, but past experience told Jofie that the bull could move in several directions, and it was possible that a marathon tracking session would be required before the bull was in sight again. Jofie turned to the others and told them that before he brought his client out from camp for a stalk, he wanted to have a better idea of just where the bull was headed next. The men agreed.

The size of the group made it impossible to remain completely silent while tracking the bull. Jofie led the group through the thorns with the game scouts and his tracker following close behind. An apprentice hunter also followed along as the group set out down the green, thorny slope into the valley where the rhino had last been seen. As the hunting party followed the rhino's spoor, the rock walls narrowed more and more until the men had to move in single file through narrow stone passages. The rhino must have barely fit through the confined space, rubbing its great gray sides on the rock faces and likely adding to an already extensive collection of scars. Finally, the canyon walls narrowed to a point where Jofie halted the group and pointed out the potential dangers of startling the rhino in the rock chasm. The spoor was very fresh, and it was entirely possible that the men would catch up to the old bull quite soon. At such close quarters, it was impossible to say if the rhino would run away or turn and charge down the canyon, driving its four-ton body toward its pursuers and leaving them helpless with nowhere to go. From now on, the hunt would require great caution. If the bull was still in the canyon, which Jofie believed it to be, a deadly confrontation remained a possibility.

Just as Jofie suspected, the old rhino was lying in a patch of thorn in one of the wider stretches of the canyon. As the men approached, the bull rose up at once, its tattered ears and narrow eyes focused on the sound. Jofie leveled his .416 rifle and watched as the rhino paused and then turned. The canyon walls echoed with the thrashing and pounding of its feet on rocks and thornbushes as the rhino made its way toward an opening at the other end of the narrow passage.

After the breathless encounter in the canyon, Jofie and his men calmed their nerves, gathered their wits, and continued on into more open country. At that point, Jofie sent for his client to join them for the duration of the stalk.

After the client arrived, the men set off again on the spoor of the rhino, this time knowing that the bull was close-by. The old rhino had kept up a steady pace for some time and then slowed, meandering in the thornscrub as it made its way up another rocky valley. When the tracks grew close together, Jofie could tell that the bull was moving slowly and had likely forgotten about the confrontation in the canyon some hours before.

With his client in tow and a caravan of rangers and trackers alongside, Jofie moved ahead through the thorns until he saw the distinctive leathery gray hide of the rhino ahead. He paused and went forward with the game rangers, who would have to verify this was indeed the old bull before the client could shoot it. It was no easy task to convince the rangers that this was the same rhino they had seen earlier. Jofie tried to explain to them that the beast lying in the thorns ahead was far too large to be anything but a massive bull rhino or an elephant, and since there were no elephants

Jofie (right), his client, and the "veteran." (Photo courtesy of Jofie Lamprecht)

on the Waterberg, the great, hulking, gray mass drowsing in the shadows ahead of them was certainly the old one-horned rhino bull. The game rangers conferred, looking again and again at the rhino up ahead and using hand signals to communicate. Since the rangers were liable for any rhino killed on the plateau, they wanted to be absolutely sure this was indeed the old bull. Finally they decided that the rhino lying hidden by the broken shadows of thorn just ahead was, in fact, the very same one they had come face-to-face with in the canyon some hours before.

Jofie motioned his client forward. Moving silently over the sand and blinking the sweat away, Jofie and his client stalked to within thirty yards of the bull. They watched it resting in the heavy thorn.

"Right there," Jofie said, pointing to the bull's ponderous silhouette in the thorns.

His client strained but saw nothing, looking at the whole of the green thornbush rather than through it. Jofie eased forward, balancing himself in a low crouch with his rifle close at hand. At twenty-five yards, the shooting sticks were set up and his client slipped his Sauer .375 Holland and Holland into place. Jofie waited. Still the man did not fire; he just watched the bush ahead.

Suddenly the rhino caught wind of the men and stood up, its bulky body moving alarmingly fast into a ready position with its head up and its tail high. Jofie swung his own rifle into position just as his client, who now had a clear view of the bull, fired a single 300-grain slug into the rhino's shoulder. As the bullet hit the heavy flesh with a dry slap, the bull turned with a grunt, which gave Jofie time to fire and hit it with a raking shot. The bush and thorn splintered under the force of the retreating bull. In a moment, all that was left was a shroud of dust raised by the retreating rhino.

The men moved forward carefully, covering the rhino's wide trail with their rifles and waiting for a short-range charge. But there was none. Eighty yards away, collapsed at full length as though in midstride, the bull lay dead on its side. Jofie slapped his client on the back and congratulated him on a job well done. As they looked the old bull over, Jofie saw the bull was as old as he had imagined, the rear horn cleanly severed and its face a road map of interconnecting scars in various stages of healing. The old bull was truly a magnificent trophy.

CHAPTER 30

INDISPOSED

Professional hunter: John Wambach
Location: Caprivi

For John Wambach and his client, the past few days had been uneventful and tiring. They were after elephants in Caprivi, and the big tuskers had managed to elude them at every turn. After many dusty miles looking for the spoor of a good bull, the men had come up empty-handed, chasing down bulls that, when they finally got close enough to evaluate them, had proven too small to shoot. Fatigue, both mental and physical, began to set in.

Large Caprivi bull moving through Namibia's northern forests. (Photo courtesy of Jacques Strauss)

Elephant herds in the Caprivi.
(Photo courtesy of Jacques Strauss)

John knew that the price of good ivory was persistence; the dusty miles, the blisters, and the spider-web scratches on the arms and legs from run-ins with wait-a-bit thorn would all be forgotten in that moment when he and his client stalked to within range of one of the big, old bulls that lived in the area. His client, having returned to hunt with John for a third time, put his faith in his professional hunter and believed that, sooner or later, they would come upon just the right elephant tracks.

Their luck changed one morning as John, his fiancée, Anneli, the hunting crew, and John's client rolled up to a water hole just after sunrise. In the first light of day the sand appeared red-brown, and glimmering flecks of quartz shimmered in the dawn like crystalline dewdrops. John's men pointed toward the far edge of the water hole. There, pressed deep into the sand, were the round tracks of several elephants. Judging from their size, they appeared to belong to large bulls. Even though the bulls had feet the size of small car tires, there was no guarantee that they were carrying good ivory, as John and his client knew all too well after many long and fruitless stalks. The only way to find out was

to catch up to the bachelor group as it moved away from the water and into the dense brush to wait out the midday heat.

John was excited for the chance to put his client on some good ivory. He motioned for his men to get down from the truck and told Anneli that he and the trackers were going to untangle the spoor and that she and the client should follow along in the hunting car on the two-track sand road. Once they had an idea of the direction the bulls had traveled, they would gather their gear and set out on foot after them.

Initially as John and his men worked down the trail, the hunting car hummed slowly behind them. After some time, John noticed that the car was no longer following. Soon it was out of sight. John and his trackers pressed on down the road, dogging the trail the trio of bulls had followed after their visit to the water hole.

Suddenly John heard the grinding of the hunting vehicle's transmission and the throaty rev of the engine as Anneli pressed down the gas pedal and brought the hunting car rapidly into view, a rising column of dust appearing behind the speeding vehicle. John and his men stopped, open-mouthed with shock at the sight of Anneli barreling down on them at highway speeds. With his rifle on his shoulder, John headed back down the road at a trot to meet the approaching car.

Anneli pulled the hunting car to the grassy edge of the road. It took a moment for John to unravel what had happened, since Anneli's explanation was frequently interrupted by excited shouts from John's white-faced client in the back of the open hunting vehicle. Eventually John gathered that the client and Anneli had come upon the bulls somewhere back down the road near where they had stopped the hunting vehicle. Based on the pallor and the excited stuttering of his hunting client, John guessed that the two had had a very personal encounter at close range with the big bulls.

While John's men gathered what supplies would be needed for the short tracking job, John tried to calm his client, who was overly excited. John rechecked his rifle and had his client do the same. If things went as planned, it might be only a matter of minutes before John's client got his chance at a big bull. John asked his client a second time about the size of the elephant. His client assured John that the elephant was very big.

It was not long before John and the others stopped in silent observation as the bulls moved slowly through the sea of green grass and squatty acacias. One of the bulls, the one closest to the men, had pretty good teeth. Its tusks were well-formed and unbroken, and like most bulls in the Caprivi and surrounding areas, the ivory was short but as thick as a man's leg. John gave a nod that meant that this bull was the one they would pursue. The men pressed forward in a silent line through the trees and thorns to set up for a shot.

The bulls were moving quickly. With the wind in their faces, the men ran after them, weaving through the outstretched tentacles of thorn as they closed the gap with the hulking gray form of the largest bull, which rolled slightly left and right as it walked through the thorns like a battleship listing slightly on a sea tide. The men slowed when they were almost in the bull's shadow, a mere fifteen yards from the looming elephant.

Close encounters with elephants can be terrifying. Being indisposed makes the confrontation all the more intense. (Photo courtesy of Jacques Strauss)

As the bull turned to its right, John readied his client for the shot. Despite the wind, which remained in the favor of the hunters, the old bull sensed something amiss and turned fully toward the hunters, its tattered ears thrust wide as it towered over the men and blocked out the sunlight. The bull was so close that it could be on top of them in a few strides, so John urged his client to shoot straight and shoot quickly.

With John backing him, the client fired, a long flash of orange blazing out from the barrel as the bullet struck home at an upward angle that would drive it through the network of bone in the elephant's forehead. The bull collapsed, its back legs folding a split second before its massive head and forequarters smashed the brush not more than a couple of large strides in front of the hunters, raising a pillar of dust and debris into the air as though an old building had been demolished with a charge of dynamite. John scanned the plains through the rising cloud of dust and saw the other bulls shuffling off out of sight. They had their elephant.

The sun sets on another day in the bush. (Photo courtesy of Jacques Strauss)

The hunters looked over the massive bull, the elephant's great tusks projecting forward like two sap-stained ivory arms reaching up toward the midmorning sun. It was an excellent trophy, and it had been thrilling to take the elephant at close quarters. Still, John wondered what had caused Elaine and his client to race the truck toward him earlier, so he asked his client what had happened.

The client smiled sheepishly as he recounted his first encounter with the elephant. Just after John and his trackers had set out to unravel the spoor on foot, the client told Anneli that he needed to answer the call of nature. He traded his heavy rifle for a roll of toilet paper and set off into the bush, looking for a comfortable place to squat not far from the road but well out of sight of the hunting car. When he had found just such a place and was marveling at the sounds of the African morning while taking care of business, he thought how odd it would be if the elephants came by right then.

Sure enough, just moments later, the elephant bulls ghosted out of the heavy cover, moving silently across the savanna. They had turned 180 degrees from the trail John was following and were moving back toward the water hole. The hunter, who was totally unarmed and woefully exposed, gathered the toilet paper, his pants, and his pride, and shuffled into thicker cover as the massive bulls loomed larger and larger, passing just beyond the place where he had, only seconds before, been blissfully imagining the irony of having a herd of elephants pass while doing what comes most naturally.

According to the client, he had finished his restroom break posthaste and scrambled back to the car, certainly frightening Anneli as he ran out of the thorns and grass with a trailing roll of toilet tissue in one hand and the look of one who has just brushed shoulders with death on his pale face. His mutterings were sufficient for Anneli to get the message: There was a big tusker in the bathroom, and it was time to go.

CHAPTER 31

The Double Take

Professional hunter: Elaine and Cornie Coetzee
Location: Central Highlands

Hosea Kutako Airport, Namibia's lifeline to the rest of the world, is incredibly small by international aviation standards. There are no jetways to carry passengers from the plane to the terminal. Upon arrival, passengers climb down from their aircraft and cross the tarmac to the small port of entry. Just inside the airport, customs officials check passports and visas before arriving passengers enter baggage claim, where a single carousel spits out luggage. Large glass doors and windows line the front of the airport and look out over miles of empty thorn savanna. In the distance, low, rocky hills, the foothills of the central highlands, rise above the shimmering green plain.

Spanish leopard hunters Pepe and Angel arrived at Hosea Kutako on the inbound flight from Frankfurt midway through the 2004 hunting season. At the airport, they met Cornie and Elaine Coetzee in the small rotunda that serves as the greeting point for nearly every hunting safari in Namibia. Cornie and Elaine are both professional hunters, both well respected and well known as the operators of CEC Hunting Safaris, based out of the capital. Cornie and Elaine greeted their newly arrived clients, gathered their bags, and set out with their usual enthusiasm to attempt something that seemed utterly impossible—taking two mature leopards in a single week.

There is perhaps no animal among Africa's lengthy list of trophy species that deserves more recognition than the leopard. Unlike the other members of the Big Five, leopards live across the vast majority of Namibia's geography, from the high, barren slopes of the Brandberg Mountains to the soggy pools of Caprivi and in every ecosystem between. Despite robust populations across much of Namibia, leopards are not easy to hunt successfully, particularly when the object of the hunt is a large, old tom. Primarily nocturnal, leopards spend the daylight hours hidden among rocks or in heavy thorn, and generally are very good at avoiding man even in areas of relatively dense human population. There are many people who have lived their entire lives in leopard country and have never seen a single cat.

Cornie and Elaine Coetzee often employed dogs in their search for leopards in the years before Namibia banned hunting with dogs in 2009. Hound hunting is a tactic that is widely misunderstood and is a polarizing topic among African PHs. Opinions vary on the use of dogs to hunt leopards, but it is without question a more physically demanding and often much more dangerous method of hunting than sitting in a blind over bait.

Elaine and Pepe with the first leopard of the safari. (Photo courtesy of Elaine Coetzee)

One great difficulty in hunting leopards with hounds is that each leopard reacts very differently to being pursued by dogs. While some leopards run and tree much like cougars in the United States, others stand and fight the dogs, sometimes injuring or killing members of the pack before the hunters arrive. The cat may stand its ground, it may try to escape, or it may charge the hunters on sight, all of which makes leopard hunting with hounds a very perilous and exhilarating way to spend your African vacation. If the cat decides to charge the hunting party, which is not particularly uncommon, it will come in a hurtling, black-and-yellow flash of fangs and exposed white claws, ready to do severe damage to approaching hunters, baying hounds, or some combination of both.

Dawn broke just after six in the morning on the second day of the hunt. Long shadows stretched over the red sand as Cornie stood outside his clients' rooms and thumped on their doors, indicating it was time for morning tea. Pepe, Angel, Cornie, and Elaine sat warming themselves in the early morning sunlight and discussed their plans for the day. Afterward, the group loaded their hunting vehicles with rifles and hounds and set out across the cold, gray savanna.

An hour after leaving camp, Elaine and Pepe split off from the group and drove over sandy roads in the central highlands not far from CEC headquarters. The idea was to find the pug marks of a big tom returning from its nightly feed and, making use of the faint morning dew, turn the dogs loose on the trail while it was still fresh enough. The concession was ideal leopard country—a series of low, rocky hills punctuating the otherwise flat veld, a tangle of weathered gray mopane mixed with waist-high, straw-colored grass. Flat-topped acacia trees scattered across the dry veld provided ideal locations for leopards to wait out the midday heat. In addition, plains game was abundant in the concession and provided the leopards with ample fare.

The hunting vehicle squelched to a stop and Elaine stepped out, walking slowly down a narrow two-track road that wound its way between patches of heavy cover. She stopped suddenly and studied a set of fresh pug marks in the drying sand. She immediately recognized the massive, rounded tracks of a tom leopard by its out-turned right front paw, the result of an injury the big cat had sustained years before. She motioned to Pepe, pointed at the spoor that led down the road ahead of them, and called the dog handlers on the radio.

It had only been a short time since the tom had crossed the road. Elaine knew that the leopard with the out-turned right paw was an old male that had lived in the concession for some time. The spoor was fresh, and the pack of dogs, a mix of blue-ticks and English foxhounds, set out in full cry along the base of the rocky hills in pursuit of the old tom as soon as they were released.

Shortly after the hounds started on the track, the leopard led them up the side of a steep, granite slope. While on the trail, Elaine and

Cornie Coetzee (left) with the second leopard. Getting one leopard during daylight hours requires tremendous luck. Getting two is very rare indeed! (Photo courtesy of Elaine Coetzee)

Pepe stumbled upon the spoor of a leopardess and her three cubs. The female leopard had made a kill not more than an hour before and was busy pulling a dead blesbok up the hillside when the hunters below had released the dogs. The tom leopard had rushed up the hillside, possibly intercepting the female and her cubs during his attempt to elude the hounds. (It was difficult to sort out the scattered and overlapping leopard prints.)

As the dogs reached the point where the leopardess had abandoned the kill, they were confused by the overlapping scent of leopards that seemed to have run in every direction. The pack would start on one track and then lose it, only to pick up another scent. Elaine, Pepe, and the dog handler arrived at the confluence of the leopard trails and found the baffled dogs running back and forth on the rocks and narrow, sandy ledges, bawling here and there as they crossed the trail of one or the other of the fleeing cats. Elaine and the handler gathered up the pack, unraveled the trail, and then led the dogs along the narrow path the male leopard had taken down the slope after he ran into the female and her cubs. When the dogs were released farther down the trail, they picked up the tom's scent and within a few moments they were once again at full cry as they ran down the slope.

After the hounds crossed the rocky crest, they picked up speed. The western slope was still in the shadows and a very thin layer of dew remained on the rocks. This held scent better than the dry east-facing slope where the tom had met the female leopard. The pack ran down the rocky face in full voice. As the sounds of the pursuing hounds faded and echoed over the distant rocks, the dog handler motioned for Elaine to swing around the mountain in an effort to catch up with the big tom.

The hunters circled the base of the hill in the hunting vehicle, spinning sand and breaking brush with the cattle guard on the front of the truck as they fought through the dry mopane. Finally, they reached the western base of the hill where they had last heard the hounds. Elaine slowed the truck and listened over the humming engine, then shifted the hunting car into gear and began climbing the slope. The Hi-Lux crept from one boulder to the next as Elaine slowly walked the two-ton vehicle up the side of the mountain while her Spanish client clung to the passenger door and watched rocks the size of rugby balls tumble end over end to the savanna below.

They stopped on a high ridge and stepped out of the vehicle to listen for the pack. The handler nudged Elaine and extended a finger toward the next ridge. There, they saw the hounds moving over car-size boulders while the cat ran ahead of them, a blur among the rocks and low trees as it led the dogs down the slope. The leopard worked its way down into the opposite valley, and they heard the pack start baying when it reached the shadowed valley. The tom had stopped to fight the pursuing dogs.

Elaine and Pepe could hear the sounds of the battle as they worked their way down the crest of the hill—the hysterical bawling of the hounds mixing with the raspy growls and roars of the leopard. There was a clatter of overturning rocks as the whole group—dogs and cat—spun in a furious cyclone of slashing claws and snapping teeth. Elaine moved Pepe into position and pointed at the tom, which had reared back on its hindquarters to face the dogs.

The leopard slashed at the dogs as Pepe fired his first shot. The bullet was not fatal, and the cat spun in midair, snarling and thrashing at the dogs as it gathered itself again. As the report of the shot reverberated among the cathedral of rocks, Elaine shouted for her client to shoot again. This time, the Spaniard's aim was true, and the cat collapsed when the rifle cracked. As the cat fell, the hounds swarmed in but stopped without touching the tom. The dogs were afraid to grab the cat, even in death.

There was a great deal of celebration at camp when Pepe and Elaine returned with the large tom. But the celebration was short-lived since Angel and Cornie still hadn't managed to find any fresh spoor during the first four days of the safari. Their luck changed on the morning of fifth day, however. The hunting party started out at dawn, driving along the sand roads that crossed the concession. The sun had not yet

Elaine with the large leopard her client took. (Photo courtesy of Elaine Coetzee)

risen above the hills to the east when Cornie stopped the truck and pointed down at the sandy ground and at a large set of pug marks pressed deeply in the sand.

The leopard had crossed the road while searching for game the night before. Cornie called over the radio for the dog handler and the trackers to meet them on the roadside. It was not long before the trackers and hound handler arrived, the dogs spilling out of the truck and milling over the fresh leopard scent under their feet. The jubilant dogs climbed over one another, their long tails slapping against the ribs of the other dogs as they worked out the trail. One by one, the dogs gave voice and disappeared in a chorus of wails and deep howls.

Cornie and the others followed the hounds and listened as the chase continued through the foothills of the highlands. Then, suddenly, the pack fell silent. Cornie and the others moved in and found the dogs scattered in heavy thornbush, trying in vain to navigate the cat's trail through the labyrinth of wait-a-bit bushes and smooth rocks. For the remainder of the day, the group worked to figure out the track, but at nightfall they relented, dusty and footsore, and returned to camp without having seen the leopard.

Cornie believed the leopard would return to the area. The next morning, the men rose and loaded the dogs while the white scythe of the moon still bathed the plains in dull blue light. By sunrise, they were back in the valley where they had lost the cat the day before. As expected, the tom had returned to the valley on its nighttime feeding route. The dogs gathered around the fresh tracks and soon fell into full voice as they rushed in a head-to-tail line on the track. Soon the dogs were out of hearing, so Cornie motioned his men into the truck and they started after the hounds and their quarry.

Word came from the dog handler, who was stationed on a high hill on the far side of the valley, that the leopard had climbed over a hill and crossed the plains beyond before finally coming to bay in a squatty shepherd's tree less than a quarter-mile away. Cornie turned to his client and translated the message, telling the wide-eyed Spaniard to keep a cool head and to be ready to shoot when the opportunity presented itself. Angel listened intently and nodded, his rifle loaded and held tightly across his chest as they worked their way over the loose rocks at the base of the hill where they had parked the truck.

Not far ahead of them, the cat hovered just off the ground and out of reach of the hounds in the low branches of the shepherd's tree. It made a rush at the dogs, grunting and growling as it slashed with its forepaws at the scrambling pack. The dogs wailed and fell back into the scattered rocks. In short order, the cat was back in the tree. One of the dogs limped away from the pack after the cat's white talons had raked its shoulder.

Cornie pulled his client close and pointed at the fork in the tree where the cat was preparing to mount another attack on the dogs. "See him? Shoot him now!"

Angel centered the rifle, controlled his breath, and squeezed the trigger. The rifle leapt up with recoil, and Cornie watched the cat tumble from the tree and land on the rocks below, scattering the dogs once more.

Cornie and Angel worked their way over the loose, khaki-colored rocks to where the big tom lay at the foot of the tree. As the handler gathered the scattered dogs, Cornie and Angel took a look at the great cat they had spent so many dusty hours chasing.

Many African hunters dream of taking a big male leopard. These elusive cats are one of Africa's most striking trophies, but connecting with a good tom takes persistence and abundant luck. Cornie's and Elaine's preparation made it possible for their clients to collect not one but two large toms in the space of a week. Even as Cornie and Elaine bid their clients farewell, plans were already underway for Angel and Pepe to return to Namibia and hunt with CEC safaris again. It was unlikely, however, that the two would ever have better luck than they had on the safari where they managed to put two big leopards in the salt in less than a week.

CHAPTER 32

The Correspondence

Hunting professional: Marina Lamprecht
Location: Windhoek

The following is a series of e-mail correspondence between a young man, an antihunter from England, and Marina Lamprecht of Hunters Namibia Safaris.

From N. Marsh, England:

I want you to know, every single one of your members is a sick %@&^. Anyone who hunts animals should be killed, brutally. I do literally hope every single one of your members gets AIDS and/or cancer. Demented *****. Go and die.

Thank you for your time.

From Marina Lamprecht, Hunters Namibia Safaris:

The rude and juvenile contents of your e-mail make it very clear to me that you are totally uninformed about the reality of the trophy-hunting industry. Also, unless you are a strict vegan, i.e., do not eat or use any form of animal products, including eggs, leather, and so on, your comments are also hypocritical. Knowing the British fondness for bacon, roast beef, and "bangers," I somehow doubt that!

My colleagues will no doubt frown upon the fact that I have even bothered to respond to such a very rude e-mail, but I do believe that you are ignorant of the facts, and, therefore, I wish to enlighten you.

Animals hunted for their trophies meet a far better end than domestic stock that are herded into pens, transported to abattoirs, and then killed, surrounded by the sight, sound, and smell of death.

Wild animals are hunted in their natural habitat and, in 95 percent of cases, are killed instantly with one shot without even knowing that the hunter is anywhere near them. What an ideal way to go!

Nightfall on safari means gathering around the fire to revisit the day's events. (Photo courtesy of Jacques Strauss)

Every inch of the animal is utilized. The skin and horns go to the trophy hunter, and the meat is used to feed local communities or is sold commercially.

Trophy hunting creates thousands of jobs and, therefore, supports thousands of families. In my own trophy hunting operation, we employ twenty people, as well as feeding 288 children at a local village school with venison from the trophy hunts. Without hunters, these children would not have regular access to protein.

If it were not for trophy hunters, wild animals in most parts of Africa would have little value to the locals and would be killed indiscriminately, as they compete with livestock (cattle, sheep, and goats) for grazing and water, as well as with human beings for agricultural land and urban development.

Last light. (Photo courtesy of Jacques Strauss)

Have you ever considered that domestic livestock are the most utilized animals on earth, and yet no one ever considers that they might become extinct? The reason is that human beings are dependent on them as an essential part of the food chain. Through trophy hunting, our wild animals are given a value, which makes them absolutely essential to the livelihood of farmers and communities. They will, therefore, be managed correctly in order to ensure their survival. As is so often the case when dealing with human beings, if it pays, it stays.

If you are a religious man, it would be clear to you that the Bible makes reference to man's right to utilize animals. Let's start in the beginning . . . Genesis 1:26: The Lord creates man in His image to be masters over all life. This is not so much directly related to my argument, but more to set up these key verses. Genesis 9:2-3: God tells Noah, after the fall of man and the flood, to further multiply and fill the earth. God placed the animals in

Noah's/man's control/power, saying, "I have given them to you as food, just as I have given you grain and vegetables."

There are many more illustrations and wordings throughout God's Word relating to the act of hunting. There are verses that mention the act of hunting and fishing. Fowling, chasing, the acts of mighty hunters, archers, the eating of wild animals, the cooking of meat, the use of bows, arrows, snares, pits, nets, decoys, using dogs to hunt, nooses, etc., are all mentioned throughout the Bible. If you take God's word as authoritative, it is clear that the hunting and partaking of meat is an accepted part of life.

So, Mr. Marsh, I urge you to reconsider your rather harsh and unfair condemnation of our industry.

Regards from our beautiful Namibia,

Marina

From N. Marsh, England:

And when have you eaten the flesh of leopards and cheetahs? Though thank you for the nice reply.

From Marina Lamprecht:

You make a very good point!

Leopards and cheetahs are indeed not usually consumed in European cultures, but they are considered a delicacy by certain African ethnic groups/tribes that also enjoy both cat and dog meat, as do the Chinese, I believe. How arrogant the "European culture" is to assume that only Western culinary traditions should be considered!

These animals are not, however, usually hunted for their meat, but for their hides. As such, you might well argue that hunting them is wrong. However, both cheetahs and leopards are carnivores and therefore cause huge losses to stock ranchers and game farmers, as they kill livestock and game animals. If they did not have the potential to generate a trophy fee paid by international hunters who wish to shoot mature males for their hides, these animals would be killed indiscriminately by these ranchers and farmers by trapping, poisoning, or shooting them, irrespective of their ages. I have heard of farmers destroying entire families of cheetahs, including cubs.

Namibia's population of these magnificent animals has been managed so well that we have been granted a CITES (Convention on International Trade in Endangered Species of Wild Fauna and Flora) quota to shoot a limited number of cheetahs as trophies. However, as the U.S. Fish and Wildlife Service does not allow the importation of cheetahs, our American hunting clients cannot take cheetah trophies home with them. As a result of this, our cheetahs do not have as much potential to generate trophy fees, and are, therefore, not "respected" by landowners and communities. As pointed out in my previous e-mail, "If it pays, it stays."

Farmers/ranchers are willing to be tolerant of losses caused by both leopards and cheetahs if they are in the position to recoup some of these

A young hunter gets accustomed to the shooting sticks, preparing for her first African hunt. (Photo courtesy of Jacques Strauss)

losses through the income generated by trophy fees for the shooting of mature animals by international trophy hunters. This leads to a situation where females and cubs are protected.

So your argument, sir, once again, is null and void.

One fact that I neglected to mention in the haste in which I wrote my previous mail is that trophy hunters want absolutely mature male animals with the largest horns. In most cases, these large males are past reproductive age, and yet their size and strength leads to a situation where they will dominate a herd of cows and keep all young, virile males out of the herd. When these mature bulls are harvested by trophy hunters, young bulls move in, and an inevitable population explosion occurs.

Also, trophy hunters invest huge amounts of money in wildlife conservation, as it is in their own best interests that all species are protected for future generations. I have yet to meet an antihunting activist who is willing to invest as generously in the protection of wildlife. These facts should give you some more food for thought.

With regards from a proudly prohunting Namibia,

Marina

From N. Marsh, England:

You do make good points, and, unfortunately, I jumped into it far too quickly. I am only seventeen, so my beliefs on this are as honed as your own; thus, my arguments may not be as good as your own.

From Marina Lamprecht:

In closing off this communication, my advice to you, young man, would be to focus on your education in the future. Please make sure that you are fully informed of the facts regarding any industry that you may choose to "attack." You have insulted many good men and women who work very hard for the good of our people and our wildlife.